Redvelations

Also by Sera Beak

Red Hot and Holy: A Heretic's Love Story

*The Red Book: A Deliciously Unorthodox Approach
to Igniting Your Divine Spark*

Redvelations

A SOUL'S JOURNEY
TO BECOMING HUMAN

SERA BEAK

sounds true
BOULDER, COLORADO

Sounds True
Boulder, CO 80306

Published 2018

Cover design by Rachael Murray
Book design by Beth Skelley

Cover image by Opie Snow Lael

Printed in South Korea

Library of Congress Cataloging-in-Publication Data
Names: Beak, Sera, 1975- author.
Title: Redvelations : a soul's journey to becoming human / Sera Beak.
Description: Boulder, CO : Sounds True, 2018.
Identifiers: LCCN 2017051575 (print) | LCCN 2018003801 (ebook) |
    ISBN 9781622039142 (ebook) | ISBN 9781622039135 (hardcover)
Subjects: LCSH: Spirituality. | Incarnation. | Reincarnation. |
    Spiritual biography. | Spiritual life.
Classification: LCC BL624 (ebook) | LCC BL624 .B3865 2018 (print) |
    DDC 204/.2—dc23
LC record available at https://lccn.loc.gov/2017051575

10 9 8 7 6 5 4 3 2 1

For Sarah,
her parents,
and all of you

Contents

The Present

Forward

Real Life   265

Acknowledgments   267

About the Author   273

Welcome

Welcome

This is my soul's story of becoming human.

It is my personal revelation (in red)
about the universal importance of recovering and embodying
the lost parts of our soul so we can become fully human
and genuinely, wildly alive.

I'm offering this revelation in an unorthodox way:

through my experiences
of remembering and reclaiming Sarah,
the forgotten daughter of Jesus and Mary Magdalene,
as the lost part of my own soul.

If your eyebrows have raised,
or you want to close this book now,
I understand.

My aim is not to convince or convert,
and you are welcome to interpret my experiences
however you wish.

What's more important than believing in *my* soul's reality
is getting up close and personal with *your* soul's reality
and doing whatever it takes to bring all of you home.

Although our soul is the truest and most essential part of us,
we *can* lose our soul, or parts of it.

In fact, soul loss is an epidemic on this planet
even, and sometimes especially, afflicting
those of us who have done a tremendous amount
of psychological and spiritual work.

Symptoms may include:

A lack of meaning, purpose,
and intimacy with ourselves.

Persistent physical ailments; emotional blocks; addictions;
harmful, stuck patterns; and unhealthy relationships.

Tendencies toward transcendence, light, and perfectionism,
and (often unconscious) avoidance of immanence, darkness, mess.

Feeling separate from and distrustful of
our bodies, each other, and Life Itself.

Difficulty knowing our truth
and expressing our unique gifts.

A haunting sense that no matter *what* we do,
something vital is still missing.

And an unremitting ache in our heart
for a Love we cannot find,
and perhaps don't believe exists,
or feel that we deserve.

Soul loss is behind many global issues we face, including:
injustice, whether political, religious, or social; violence; disease;
excess consumerism; and the ever-growing environmental crisis.

Which is one reason why I wrote this book:
to do my small part in helping
to improve and ease this hurting earth.

Here's the other reason:

When I turned thirty-four years old,
it became frighteningly clear
that if I did *not* embody my soul,
I could not continue living.

While I put up quite a fight,
eventually I chose to Live.

I chose to undergo the mysterious process
of embodying my soul and becoming human,
part of which required that I remember and reconcile
my experiences of Sarah and share them in this book.

Although my particular process and soul's story may appear
more unusual than some, its themes of

love and loss,
betrayal and forgiveness,
suffering and healing,
death and resurrection,

are part of *every* human's experience.

In fact, *being human* is a wound and a trauma we all share.
And yet, it is by embodying our soul and thereby becoming *fully human*
that we can help heal ourselves and this planet.

Embodying our soul involves purposefully entering our wounds
and facing, feeling, and embracing all parts of ourselves
as well as the dark luminosity of Life.

Embodying our soul entails valiantly wrestling
our divinity to the ground
and spreading our humanity all over the place.

Embodying our soul and becoming human is *how*

Love lands
here
and transforms
here.

And it is, I believe,
why we are here.

It ain't easy.
Incarnation takes work.

It takes blood, sweat, and tears;
a wicked sense of humor;
outrageous courage;
and a heaping dose of devotion
to Something
our minds might not ever understand.

Unfortunately, due to dire conditions on this planet,
soul work has become a privilege, and therefore a responsibility
for those of us who have the time and means to do it.

I am aware of my privilege,
and I take my responsibility seriously.

I know that everything we do for our soul
supports all souls and this earth.

In other words, soul work is a form of activism.

It's a movement toward wholeness
that we make together.

Therefore, *Redvelations* is more than a book
about my personal journey toward wholeness.

It's a raw Call to a rare kind of action.

It's a fiery Reminder
of the absolute necessity
and indomitable power
of *your* soul.

It's an open-handed offering
respectfully placed
on the often-overlooked
Altar of Our Humanity.

It's an honoring of the Lineage of Life
and a testament of True Love.

More intimately,

Redvelations

is
my
heart

smashed

onto
pages.

Handle with care.

Cautions

Redvelations is not a light read
because the soul is not a light thing.

There are suggested "breaks,"
but follow your body's lead.

I swear. Swear words and soul work
go hand in hand, for me.

What I share in this book
is not intended
to diagnose or treat others.

When working with past trauma,
a safe and secure environment
and a strong support team are needed.

Redvelations shares an intimate relationship
between a man and a woman.

I also use the labels: "Divine Masculine" and "Divine Feminine,"
"father" and "mother," and the binary pronouns "he" and "she."

Rather than interpret this literally or as heterosexism,
I encourage you to focus on the *metaphoric* meaning

and the contrary, but mutually supportive, aspects we *all* contain,
no matter our sexual preference, sex, gender(s), or beyond.

Bringing these universal aspects together
within us

shatters all restrictions
to Love,
and creates and sustains Life.

Soul Speak

The fluctuating voice and prose-in-verse format of *Redvelations*
are not literary devices, dramatic affects, poetic posturing,
spiritual performance, or method (like channeling).

In "The Past" part of the book
I allowed my soul to speak in her native tongue,
which is not limited by time or historical language or references.

In "The Present" part of the book
I allowed my humanity and my divinity
to collide in my body
and I wrote from their meeting place.

The Soul's Reality

Redvelations comes from
my lived experiences, my body,
and my soul's memories.

I used no outside sources (save the quote below),
only inner Sources.

You might want to know more details
than are provided in "The Past,"
but my soul shared only what she needed to.

Many of my soul's memories contradict
what we have been taught as history.

Expressing our soul
exposes a Reality
that can upset the reality
we have subscribed to
and collectively agreed upon.

The soul does not rely upon evidence,
facts, or rationality.

The soul cares less about what you think
and more about what you feel.

The soul's reality
doesn't make a lot of sense,
but it makes a lot of Love.

Much of this book takes place in the soul realm.
The soul realm contains our past, present, and future.

It is where I remember my past experiences,
locate and heal my core wounds, process my feelings,
resource my innate wisdom, release trauma from my body,
and reconnect with and retrieve fragmented pieces of my soul.

I do not use techniques, special abilities, practices, or tools
like hypnosis, psychic powers, meditation, or hallucinogens
to enter or work within the soul realm.

I simply and soberly
sink into my body,
ground into the earth,
and open my heart.

The soul realm is easily accessible.
It blazes inside each and every one of us
and permeates the physical reality outside of us.

It's *Organic* Reality.

In her brilliant book *The Meaning of Mary Magdalene*,
Cynthia Bourgeault describes this realm as follows:

> It is a realm that objectively exists . . . and it is from this realm
> that our human sense of identity and direction ultimately derive. . . .
> However one names it, the point to keep uppermost in mind
> is that it designates a sphere that is not less real but more real
> than our so-called objective reality and whose generative energy
> can change the course of events in the world.

Put differently: the soul realm is just as real
as our external or material reality,
and, some say, even more real.

Whether we are aware of it or not,
we are profoundly influenced by this realm
because before, after, and beyond our body
we are a soul.

When we consciously enter this realm,
we can connect intimately with our soul,
and all souls, including the Soul of this Universe.

Therefore, our experiences in the soul realm
are both personal and universal.

And, what we do in this realm directly impacts
our daily lives, our bodies, humanity,
and this entire planet.

In other words, what happens in the soul realm
doesn't stay in the soul realm.

It affects All of Life.

Soul Authority

I do not believe we need
any more spiritual authorities
telling us what The Truth is.

However, I have learned that it is
extremely important to allow the soul
to express *its* truth with authority.

Especially if the soul has been silenced
for a long time, like mine has.

In *Redvelations* I have (finally) allowed
my soul to speak her truth with authority
about such things, like

Who We Are, Where We Come From, Why We Are Here,
and the Nature of Reality in this Universe.

I have also (finally) allowed my soul to share
her experience of Jesus and Mary Magdalene,
and her perspective on their teachings.

While I honor and champion
your spiritual authority,
reality, and truth,

it's time for me to share my own.

You may not like my soul's truth,
or agree with it, or believe in it,
and you don't have to,

but I believe that when *any* soul
dares to express its truth,
it deserves respect
and a reception in the heart.

A Technical Note:
I use a capital *S* to indicate the Divine Soul,
a lowercase *s* to indicate the human soul,
and a capital *S* when I'm referring to them *both*,
which will be apparent in context.

A Map

Redvelations starts backward
at the very beginning of my Soul's
journey into this Universe,

then provides a brief metaphysical orientation
and spiritual baseline for the rest of the book,
including a fundamental overview of what I refer to
as the "cosmic dimension."

Initially, *Redvelations* is more abstract and informative.

In "The Past" my perspective becomes more personal
as I share Sarah's life.

"The Past" occasionally reads like an unconventional sermon
but mostly like a bittersweet love story that isn't afraid of the dark.

The writing shifts in "The Present" (more swear words and humor),
as I transparently struggle with what is shared in "The Past"
and question and doubt my experiences.

"The Present" is also where I do the gritty,
yet gratifying, work
of retrieving and embodying my soul.

You may prefer the first half of this book,
or you may prefer the second half.
However, *both* halves make the Redvelation whole.

As for the complex and provocative phenomenon of "past lives,"
well that's a subject for a different book,
and the need to return to past lives is specific to each soul.

But for me, I *couldn't* move forward in this life
until I went backward.

So, with that, let's go Backward.

Backward

The Beginning

I have no Beginning
but I've had a beginning
in *this* Universe.

Essentially
I am my own Universe.
As are you.

As a Universe, I once heard
an indescribably beautiful
Love Song

coming from *this* Universe
—the one you and I are currently inhabiting—

inviting Us All
to experience and express
Ourselves *inside of It.*

For, this is what we Universes do.

We brush up against each other,
enter each other,
and engage in intimate Relationship.

We are necessary participants
in each other's evolution.

This Universe sang about intriguing things, like:

birth and death,
masculine and feminine,
light and dark,

organic and synthetic,
pleasure and pain,
cherry pie and chipmunks.

Forgetting,
and
falling
apart.

Remembering,
and
coming
back
together.

In other words:
It sang the Song of Itself.

And, as you know,

It
is

SPECTACULAR!

I responded instantaneously,
the way a Universe can't help but respond
when it has met its Evolutionary Match.

And, I projected a fractal
of *my* Universal Being
into *this* Universal Being,

where I experienced
a Love
unlike any other.

This Universe had split Itself into Two:

A Divine Masculine
and
a Divine Feminine

so It could

Make Love with Itself
and give birth to Us.

One *and* Two
created a Third.

I contain all the qualities of this Universe,
but I maintain *my own* Universe's Essence,

which in this Universe
manifests as
RED.

Red is a name for the part of me
that is eternal, infinite, connected to
All That Is,
but also utterly unique.

Red is my sacramental signature
in the Book of Life,
and my sacrificial offering
in this Love Story.

Red is my Divine Soul.

You too have a Divine Soul
with your own significant signature
and unmatched offering.

You too are a distinct Divine Being,
in Essence equal to but different from
the distinct Divine Being of *this* Universe.

This Truth of Who We Are
has been repeatedly forgotten
but always Known.

It has been
buried
inside us.

It's the foundation of our Journey
away from Ourselves
and now
back Home to Ourselves.

Remembering and Reclaiming
Ourselves is imperative.

For, *our own* Universe's Essence
is what *this* Universe
desires and needs
in order to become Itself.

And, we desire and need
this Universe's Essence
in order to become Ourselves.

It is a reciprocal Relationship.
It is a Living Love.

It is a Holy Harmony
that we can only play
Together.

There is a simpler way to view this.

Our human parents created us
—a physical baby with their genes, traits,
and perhaps sense of humor—

but our parents did not
create our *soul.*

Similarly, our Divine Parents
came together to create our Body
in this Universe,

but they did not create our Divine Soul,
which is a fractal of an already existing Universe.

Our Divine Parents want us to offer
Something new to their Universe,
and be Ourselves *with* Them.

A few Family Snapshots:

The Father and the Mother
and
the Child
(who is becoming an Adult).

The Divine Masculine and the Divine Feminine
and
the Divine Soul.

The Creator and the Creatrix
and
the Creatives.

No matter how you view
Us,

We are

A
Trinity
of
True
Love.

The Separation

After we enter this Universe,
we continue to project parts of our Divine Soul
into each dimension of this Universe

so we can experience everything
that this magnificent place has to offer
and learn and live as much as possible.

The projected part of our *Divine Soul*
that currently has a body on this earth
can be called our *human soul.*

It is the part of our Divine Soul
that is incarnate on the third dimension.

However, there are several dimensions between
our Divine Soul and our human soul.

We are multidimensional Beings
who stretch deep and wide.

But with each denser dimension
we enter as a soul,

we feel further and further away
from our Divine Soul,
and from the Creator and the Creatrix,

who *Together*
form our Home Base.

We forget Who We Are,
Where We Come From,
and Why We Are Here.

To add to this feeling of disunion,
we fragment into even more "separate" soul pieces
due to certain experiences.

We not only "lose" our Divine Soul
but we can also "lose" our human soul,
or pieces of it.

The Good News:

No matter how far we might have strayed,
or how fragmented and lost we might feel,
we are never unreachable by our Own Arms.

While we as Divine Souls
have purposefully spread Ourselves
across this entire Universe,

there comes a point during our journey
when it is Time
to reintegrate our pieces.

This enigmatic and sacred process
of embodying all aspects and dimensions
of our Soul *in our body*

is called Incarnation.

It is how we become fully human.
It is how we come Home, *here.*

This process entails

Remembering
that we are a Soul,

recognizing how
and learning why
we lost our Soul,

and then, retrieving,
healing,
and embodying our Soul.

While there are countless ways we lose our Soul,
the most paradoxical and overlooked ways
are through religion and spirituality.

The Cosmic Dimension

In order to understand why and how we lose our Soul
through religion and spirituality,

we need to take a closer look at what I will call
the cosmic dimension or realm.

This is the largest dimension
in this Universe,
but far from the deepest,
and it penetrates this planet.

The cosmic dimension is where
religions; spiritual systems; new-age paradigms;
most masters, guides, gods, and goddesses; heavens (and hells);
certain enlightened states of consciousness;
and even what appear to be entire *universes* exist.

Oppositional, synthetic, and nefarious
forces and beings also reside in the cosmic realm.
These interfering forces and beings provide souls
with exceptional tests and outstanding challenges.

Oppositional forces and beings
seem to operate "against" us.

Synthetic forces and beings
are counterfeits of Organic Life.

Nefarious forces and beings
sometimes appear "dark" or "evil,"
but they can also appear "light" and "divine,"
often blindingly so.

Ultimately, everything in the cosmic dimension
serves a Sacred Purpose
and is necessary for our growth.

It's where and how we get to
explore and experience
innumerable

spiritual realities and possibilities
for epochs of "time,"

most notably what it is like
to forget, disclaim,
give away, and lose

our Sovereignty,
Distinct Divine Identity,
and Soul.

But

there is a Wilder,
Simpler,
and more Organic

Reality

and

Way of Being

Alive

in this Universe

that

pulses
behind

and

winks
through

this colossal dimension.

It is this Organic Reality
and Natural Way of Being
that my first human family
came from and demonstrated.

It Calls us Home.

Not to Source, not to Oneness, not to Consciousness,
not to god and goddess or a deity,
not to a billion other realms or cosmic experiences
or even enlightenment,

but to Ourselves.

This is the Lineage I come from.
Every Soul belongs to It.

A Beginner

I've had many manifestations
and many experiences
on many different dimensions.

But, I'm a bumbling beginner at becoming human.

It's the hardest but most important thing
I have ever attempted to do.

Ever.

And, it is the mission of my Lineage.

So, let's begin my story of becoming human.

The Past

Conception

I Remember when True Love called me to Earth.

It was an ecstatic invitation to Incarnate
created between Him and Her.

It was a reunion of what once was,
a conscious conception of what will be,

a beloved and familiar beckoning,
but now from physical reality.

Two became One to form a Third.

The nature of True Love
burning between my first parents
matched the color of my Soul:

Red.

Becoming human allowed me
to be with my Family,
in a remarkable new way.

It was in our bodies and through our humanity
that we would resurrect Life on Planet Earth.

Freedom would happen the only way it can:

not from the outside-in or the top-down,
but from the inside-out and the ground up.

Granite to galaxies,
fingernails to feathers,
dirt to deities.

How would we do what had never been done before?

Love.

It would be a Revelation
that could start a Revolution.

I chose my role in the Revolution.
I *was* my role in the Revelation.

Becoming human was a guaranteed growth spurt,
a sanctified part of the Original Plan,

and a necessary
but unpaved path
Home.

To Live
as
Divine *and* Human
is

True Love's
Ultimate
Dare.

And I bravely took It.
As did you.

The Body

Entering her womb
was like entering an embrace.

Warmth wrapped around me,
gently squeezing
the infinite into finite.

Life made so many
movements
and sounds,
in so little space.

Her rhythmic heart beat:

Ba Boom Ba Boom Ba Boom

The steady inhale and exhale of her lungs:

whoosh (expand), *phoosh* (contract)

The gurgling of her organs:

badoolp, gadoolp, wadaloop

The blood rushing through her veins:

huuuuuuuusssshhhhh

Her female body,
like Her planetary Body

welcomed
All of Me
here.

Merging with my embryonic body
was like nothing I had ever experienced before
in the entire Universe.

My growing body had a consciousness all its own,
a primal wisdom native to the earth
mixed with the consciousness of my parents

that filled every multiplying cell,
organizing the raw materials of human life
with exquisite precision,
delicate detail,

and careful preparation
for what was coming in:

my Soul.

The desire for this union was unmistakable.

My Divine Soul
reverentially
reached
through the dimensions

toward my human body,
like a lover reaches for their beloved.

And, I felt my new body
respond naturally to this adoration
by opening effortlessly,
like a flower welcoming the sun.

While my awareness extended
outside my mother's body,
my point of reference
became my body,

and my access
to Remembrance
was through the

red,
beating
heart of me.

Having a human body felt intense,
to say the least.

Still, it was celestially and cellularly clear that
there is nothing behind incarnation,
but Love.

My Parents

The first human other than myself
that I fell in love with
was my mother.

Then
my father.

I never met my father outside my mother's womb,
and this was later held against me.

But, I knew my father from the body of my mother,
the human he was closest to and loved with all his heart.

I remember the way my environment changed
when my father was near.

My mother's temperature rose.
Her heart sped up and spilled out.

Everything whirling inside her

fell
into
place.

While she was complete on her own,
she was home with him.

My mother was acutely attuned to my father.

She could tell if he had slept well the night before,
had eaten enough that day,
or had an argument with a friend.

She sensed his moods,
his thoughts,
his innermost feelings.

She knew his strengths and his weaknesses,
and she carried his certainty and his doubts
alongside her own.

She was his Soul's Other Half.

Her connection to him didn't falter,
even when they were separated

by a crowd,
a desert,
a death.

My mother knew my father in every way one can know another,
but it was through her heart that she knew him best.

And, the attentiveness my father gave my mother
demonstrated that he knew and loved her
as she knew and loved him.

Despite what others believed,
I knew my father,
intimately.

I knew the vibration of his voice,
the transmission of his touch,
the heat of his Soul's Fire.

I recognized his movements
and felt their impact.

I tossed about upon
the waves he created.

I sensed how much
he longed to be understood,
but so rarely was.

I did not, and I still do not,
know everything about him,
nor do I entirely understand him.

But he was my father.
And I was honored to feel his heart
beat so close to my own.

While initially I was a planned secret,
my growing presence hidden and unknown by others,
my father never let me feel unknown by him.

His love for me was as present and palpable as hers.

Almost every night,
my father's warm hands found
my mother's barely swelling belly.

Nothing felt safer or surer than

Him
holding
Her
holding
me.

Our three hearts beating together.

Their Love

My time with both my parents
was brief.

But, it was enough.

It was enough to *never* forget
what was shared between them.

I remember their mindful conversations
and mindless chattering.

I remember their belly-shaking laughter,
and their tears that felt like

they came from,
and flowed back into,

every body of water on this planet.

I remember their fights
and their farts,

their ferocity
and their tenderness,

their rough edges
and their smooth lines,

but most of all,

I remember the pervasive
Truth of Their Togetherness.

My parents delivered
a desperately needed nutrient
into the soil of this planet
and into the soil of our souls:

True Love

The Love my parents shared
was felt by all
but understood by few.

It was as strong as the Sun
and as solid as the Earth.

It created a Field of Remembrance

that both excited
and upset
those around them.

Their Love was a Force
to be reckoned with . . .

and still is.

Through Each Other

There was no hiding or seeking
between my Parents.
They were found through each other.

They *are* found through each other.

You cannot fully know and love my father
unless you know and love my mother.

You cannot fully know and love my mother
unless you know and love my father.

And, without knowing and loving them
knowing and loving
each other,
you cannot know and love me.

You cannot know and love the Soul.

Divine in Body

Like all souls of a fetus,
my awareness stretched beyond the womb
and into the lives of my parents.

My father was known for many things,
but one was his gift for Healing.

However, the only miracle he ever performed
was the startling demonstration of
being fully Alive.

Around such Aliveness
that which has died inside of us
will be brought back to Life,

Naturally.

Place your bare feet on the earth
or your opened palm upon a tree,
and you will start to feel better,
no matter what your ailment.

The earth and the tree are not healing you.
They are Reminding you of What You Are.

My father's full-bodied Presence shouted:

I Know Who You Are!
I *Love* Who You Are!

REMEMBER
YOURSELF

and

LOVE
YOURSELF!

COME BACK TO LIFE!

Be aware of putting "other gods"
before What Lives inside you.

We are meant to give and receive
support, healing, and love,

but if we put something or someone
before our own Soul,

including my father,

we have missed his most fundamental teaching.

My father was devoted to *his* Divine Soul,
whom he called "Father,"
and is the Creator of *this* Universe,
and therefore our "Father" as well,

and my father was devoted to the distinct Divine Soul
within every human,
who is the Creator of Its *own* Universe.

My father brought the Divine Masculine to Earth
and humans to their divinity
by being himself.

There was nothing he did that you can't do
if you trust and love your Divine Soul
and the Divine Soul of this Universe.

Body in Divine

My mother Healed in a similar, but different, way.

While my father focused on the Divine living within the body,
my mother focused on the Body living within the divine.

Her devotion was to *her* Divine Soul,
whom she called "Mother"
and is the Creatrix of *this* Universe,
and therefore our "Mother" as well,

and she was devoted to *all* Universes
Who were incarnate.

Under her loving hands,
she reminded the body
that it was the Beloved.

She raised the Soul to the surface of the skin,
realigned the bones with the Being,
and teased the tissues into their Truth.

She reopened a closed body
to the wisdom and power
of feeling.

She taught pleasure as a path
and gave pain a safe place to rest.

She wept with those who needed tears
and laughed uproariously with those
who needed (bawdy) jokes.

She demanded respect and fair treatment of girls,
encouraged their studies, intuition, and independence,
and delighted in their rowdy play.

She reminded women
that the blood flowing out of them each cycle
fed the earth,

and was one of many physical signs
that they were Creatrixes
who had the power to generate Life,

and when women stopped bleeding,
they contained and increased
their Creative Power
and could steward it as they chose.

My mother reclaimed the human body
and revered the planetary body,
as parts of *Her* Body.

My mother brought the Divine Feminine to Earth,
and Souls into the body,
by being herself.

There is nothing she did that you cannot do
if you trust and love your body
and the Body of this Universe.

Side by Side

My mother's public presence next to my father
declared that there can be no real Kingdom
without a true Queendom

and that the human body
was the entrance to them both.

My parents' balanced relationship
challenged the presiding power models,
which dictated that a woman's place
was behind or beneath a man,
not by his side.

My mother was born in the north
and brought to my father's land as a child servant,
which added to her otherness.

Therefore, my mother was often mistreated
not only by those who opposed the Revolution,
but even by some who were a part of it.

Beware of those who transcend, reject, dominate, or devalue
the earth, the body, the other, and the feminine.

They are doing the opposite of what my father did.

Likewise, be aware of those who idolize
only the body and the earth.

This is not how my mother lived.

My mother loved, respected, and honored my father
because she loved, respected, and honored her own masculine.

My father loved, respected, and honored my mother
because he loved, respected, and honored his own feminine.

They were One in themselves,
which allowed them
to become One with each other.

Remember,
we are here to hold the hands
and the hearts
of *both* our Divine Parents.

Sexuality

I remember how my mother's skin
responded to my father's touch;
how her body bloomed against his.

I remember how her uterus contracted with pleasure
as her heart expanded with purpose.

I remember how every part of her
was worshipped
by every part of him.

Love was Made
frequently and freely,
without hesitation or holding back.

My parents had no advanced sexual training
nor practiced esoteric techniques.

They were Naked,
thus fully Revealed.

Every part of themselves
available to Touch.

They were receptive to the guidance of every sensation,
awake to the intelligence of their human desires,
and surrendered to Life Loving through them,
as them.

Ecstasy couldn't help
but fall from their laps
into ours.

While who we Love
is uncontrollable,
and how we Love,
limitless,

my parents
were sexually intimate
with each other,
and with each other alone.

This is not a moral principle.
This was mystical physics.

It was in the container of my parents' commitment
that Life's erotic charge became *highly* concentrated,
creating explosive change on this planet.

The synthetic sexual paradigm makes the male
disconnect and drift, never satisfied by one,
constantly craving shallow stimulation
and avoiding feminine depths.

His wanderlust and unavailability
focus on achievement, spirituality, warring,
and his desire to be anywhere but

Here,
with
Her

are socially supported and accepted
as part of his biology.

He is excused as "just being a man."

The synthetic sexual paradigm keeps the female
distracted and insecure,
never satisfied with her body or her life,
constantly comparing and competing with other women,
avoiding true masculine strength.

Her worth is locked into her looks,
domestic skills, mothering, and productivity,
and the resulting instability, depletion, and need to control
are reinforced by the culture and accepted as part of her biology.

She is excused as "just being a woman."

So, we have a man never satisfied by a woman,
a woman never satisfied by herself,
and a planet that is being destroyed as a result.

There is *nothing* Natural about this.

We each have an organic masculine and a synthetic masculine,
an organic feminine and a synthetic feminine.

Discerning their differences
inside and outside of us
is an ongoing practice.

The organic masculine honors, supports, and protects
the organic feminine
that is attempting to re-emerge from every human.

The organic feminine honors, supports, and inspires
the organic masculine
that is attempting to re-emerge from every human.

And together, they honor, support, and protect the Earth.

Unfortunately, synthetic sexuality reigns.

That which was meant to unify us
mostly separates us.

That which was meant to heal us
often harms us.

That which was meant to adore and awaken the body
is used to shame and abuse the body.

That which was meant to express and celebrate Life
now censors and condemns Life.

Organic Sexuality
is our Original Innocence,
not our original sin.

And, it is not, nor ever was,
meant to be shared *only* between
a man and a woman.

Close your eyes.

Place one hand on your body
and one hand on the earth.

Feel.

The Erotic is a Divine Force
humming all around you
and through you.

It is Life madly in Love with Itself.

We must
Touch
Life

and

be
Touched
by
Life

in order to
hummmmmmmmmmmmmmmmmmmm
again.

Marriage

Marriage was an essential teaching
and ardent practice of my parents.

Marriage is not a contract,
a set of laws,
a social custom,
a religious tradition,
or only between a male and a female.

It is a Unification of Being

that materializes when
the masculine and the feminine,
the body and the soul,
the dark and the light,
and all contrasts
come together.

It transforms our lead into everyone's gold.

Marriage can happen alone,
but my parents chose
to marry one another.

It was through the trials and triumphs
of intimate relationship
that my parents practiced and attained

REUNION.

My parents came together and stayed together
not just to better and become themselves
but also to contribute to
Something Greater than themselves:

LIFE.

Everything they did together,
they did for every living thing.

No matter how difficult life was
they did not abandon
this earthly reality.

Our Parents
were Committed
to
Being here.

They were
Devoted
to
Loving here.

They
Married
here.

To separate the earth from the divine,
the body from the soul,
the sexual from the sacred,
the Queen from the King

is an old game
that we Beings
once agreed to play.

My parents' relationship announced:

GAME OVER!

Those who wanted the game to continue
divorced my father from my mother,
made him celibate, her a whore,
and aborted their child.

By making Him the only Way,
they have led us down a one-way street
to a broken home.

But, if you open the door
and dance in the fertile fields,

you will Remember
the Original Partners.

You will Remember that this Universe
is an Intimate Relationship.

Relationship is What It's All About.

Our Parents' Marriage
is our Primary Memory.

It's proven through every particle in Creation.

It clamors through every cell,
and shouts from every soul:

COME UNION!

Fully Human

Despite their Divine Origins,
my parents were not perfect.
They were fully human and flawed.

As their child, I knew this more than most.

While my parents were there for each other
and for the whole wide world,
they weren't there for me when I needed them most.

Like all humans in relationship,
my parents hurt those closest to them
and made mistakes.

Sometimes they allowed
their wounds to wipe away their wisdom,
their shadows to shuffle their path,
their fears to fumble their footsteps.

Sometimes, their divinity diminished their humanity,
or their humanity devoured their divinity.

Sometimes, they would let the crowds and the conditions,
the darkness and the desperation,
overtake them.

Sometimes they wished every person on this planet would go away
and every Soul in this Universe would leave them alone.

Sometimes they wished for any other life but their own.

Many don't want to know this about my parents.

For we have been taught to idealize my parents,
to worship them, emulate them,
not roll around in the mud *with* them.

But perfection is a trap,
especially spiritual perfection.

It punishes us for *being us*,
and lures us away from Living.

It's a siren's song
that breaks our soul
upon the rocks.

My parents' faults free us
from the righteous, the rigid,
and the superior.

Their imperfections relay
a Way of Living and Loving
that is more Holy than any other.

My parents punched a hole in heaven
and dragged divinity to the earth.

They broke spiritual laws
by following Natural Lore.

They replaced impenetrable, shiny icons
with their vulnerable, scarred flesh.

They roughed up religious romanticism
with human reality.

They got their hands dirty and their hearts broken.
They punctuated their prayers with swears.

They were *Real.*

My parents experienced and expressed
both
their divinity and their humanity.

If they prioritized one over the other
(if we prioritize one over the other)

they would be incomplete
(we will be incomplete)

and so would be their mission
(and so will be our mission).

This is what being *fully* human means.

It is the combination
that unlocks and frees
this entire Universe.

Oppositional forces have separated
our Father from his humanity
and our Mother from her divinity,

sentencing us to
either or.

When they are
Remembered
as *both*

we will more readily
accept and love ourselves
as we are.

Then, the Revelation will be recovered.
And the Revolution, unstoppable.

Interfering Forces

My parents discerned
and dealt with
interfering beings and forces.

My parents exorcised nefarious beings,
stood up to oppositional forces,
but exposed what was synthetic

by being unbound
and unprocessed
themselves.

You can too.

Using your body and soul as guides,
you can respectfully sift through teachings
from every tradition and dimension
on (and off) this planet,

and *sense* what is organic
and what has been exposed to pesticides
or molded into an unnatural shape.

You can rediscover:

What includes you
and what removes you.

What separates you
and what unifies you.

What overpowers you
and what empowers you.

What pulls you out of your body
and what sinks you into it.

What is excessively sweet
and what is appropriately salty.

What is stiff and what is flexible.
What evolves and what stays the same.
What is colorful and what is black and white.
What cherishes differences and what curbs diversity.
What judges and what seeks to understand.

What makes you laugh
and what keeps you serious.

What sparks your sovereignty,
and what spanks it.

What treasures your truth,
and what tramples it.

What cages your wild,
and what encourages your

RRRRRRROOOOOOOOAAAAAARRRRR!!!!

What loves,
and what
Loves.

You will Know by Being
and Trusting Yourself.

When discerning our Lineage,

feel for the Real.

Our Lineage feels like your hand in fresh soil.

Messy,
nourishing,
grounding,
and available to all.

Our Lineage *is* Life.

The Garden of Life

After a day's work,
even during difficult times,
my parents made sure to celebrate

often, with dear friends,
delicious food, fine wine
and exuberant dancing till dawn.

But when they wanted
to be alone together,
they came to this garden.

Romps and rolls happened here.
Weeds and wonder.
Conversations that made the stars lean closer.

I remember once in this garden,
my mother started to move

from
the core of the earth,
HERSELF.

My father's heart met the ground
at my mother's muddy feet.

I remember once in this garden,
my mother released her rage toward the patriarchy
in ways that would terrify the fiercest armies,

till she finally collapsed,
spent and sobbing in my father's open arms,
where forgiveness found and freed her.

I remember once in this garden,
my mother led my father into his shadow lands,
where he howled and heaved

as what was covered
became uncovered

and what was separate
became joined.

My father's teachings were never the same after that.

I remember once in this garden,
in the midst of a serious debate,

my mother leapt up
startling both my father and me,

lifted up her robes,
and shook
her fleshy bottom.

It was a bare transmission that needed no words.
My father laughed so hard the trees shook.

I remember more than once in this garden
joyful musings about me.

What would I be like? Whom would I resemble more?

Would I have my mother's hot temper and blue eyes
and my father's sense of humor and dark skin?

Would I share Our Love as a Way of Life?

The whole word felt pregnant with our possibility.

More than events or conversations
in this garden,

I remember moments
shared between them.

Moments so pure
they refuse words.

A look.
A touch.
A nod.
A wink.
A sigh.

These untranslatable moments
are imprinted on my soul.

They tenderize my pain with gratitude
for my once-beloved place in her soft belly.

They remind me that not all went to waste.

This garden,
like few other places,
held Us Together.

If you Love
with your
Whole Body,

you too

will re-enter
this Garden
of Life.

Changes

The energy around me had been escalating for weeks.

Voices were clipped,
opinions strong,
and emotions charged.

My mother's heartbeat raced
and her stomach churned.

She wasn't eating much,
and what she was eating
wasn't digesting properly.

She got sick at the last community meal,
raising suspicions that she was with child.

But her sickness wasn't due to me.
Her body was rejecting what was forthcoming.

My mother held onto my father
with a fierceness
that couldn't quite
cover her fear,

and my father held my mother
like he was trying
to bring her body
into his breaking heart.

My whole world was changing,
and I did not understand why.

Whatever was happening
didn't feel good to her body
or my body.

It didn't feel Good to *any* Body.

The Garden of Death

This particular night in the garden felt different.
The garden didn't respond to us the way it normally did.

The ground under my mother's feet felt tight with tension.
The animals stayed at a distance.
Even the air seemed to be holding its breath.

It felt like we were hanging over a cliff.

I didn't know that this was the last night
we would be together as a family.

I didn't know that I was about to lose my father.

But my mother did.

She tucked her grief away,
as far away as possible,

because if she allowed herself to feel it then,
there would be no strength to hold us later.

Everything was communicated in their last embrace.

Everything
they
shared
Together

as

a

Universe
folded
into
flesh.

When she finally broke from their embrace
and walked away,

the garden wilted and wept
as all living things do

when a life is taken too soon
and a Love Story comes to an end.

The Darkest Day

I am at the foot of a cross.

My mother's body is wrapped around
this unforgiving wooden structure,

and she is wailing
with the force
of a hurricane.

Her throat is raw,
her head is pounding,
her skin is splintered.

Her bodily liquids are mixed with his.

Directly above us,
my father's body is writhing in agony
and shaking from shock.

Everything he is,
everything he attempted to do,
is pouring down
over us.

No matter what the guards do,
my mother won't let go;
she won't let go;

she
won't
let
go.

She is hanging onto this cross
like it is the only thing keeping the earth spinning on its axis,
like it is the last ray of truth touching this planet,
like it is the only way to keep my father alive.

But my father is dying
in the most horrifying way,
surrounded by a cruel crowd,
betrayed by those he trusted.

There is little separation
between what he is feeling,
what my mother is feeling,
and what I am feeling.

I am *lost* in feelings.

But, the foremost feeling is

PAIN.

It batters my small body
and the body of the one
who is responsible for me.

It paints my family portrait in black.

But it is not just a personal
and familial pain I feel,
it is also

a
Pain
that hammers
through
the
Hands and Feet
of
Life
Itself.

My parents don't soothe me
or make this Pain go away.

I feel abandoned,
helpless,
unsure if I can survive.

I expand my awareness,
desperately searching
for some kind of external support,

but all I encounter
is chaos, terror,

and the broken remains
of our community's noble intentions.

The men in our group have run away,
fearing they are next.

Only a few brave women have stayed,
not caring if they are next.

My father's mother is one of them.

I reach out to my grandmother for comfort,
but she is gutted by grief
and all the feelings that come from
watching one's child be brutally murdered
in broad daylight.

Everyone and everything
is breaking down around me.

As my beloved father exhales for the last time,
my beloved mother inhales everything left behind,
and I receive the final blows from a ruthless reality:

"*This* is what happens when you become human.
This is how the world responds when True Love Incarnates.
This is life in a body on Earth."

My heart smashes into a million red pieces.

Wounded to the core,
I respond exactly how I feel:

"I want no part of *This*."

The Sell

Abruptly, a light
infiltrates the darkness.

A luminous being approaches me
with open arms and comforting words:

"Oh my poor dear one,
this is all so terrible and terrifying indeed,

but it is also to be expected
when you have a Soul such as yours.

Your Redness is why everyone,
including your parents,
have abandoned you.

But I am here.
I can keep you safe.
Let me take away your suffering.

All you have to do is give up your futile mission
and give me the very thing that puts you and others in danger,
and creates so much pain:

your Soul."

I do.

I give my Soul to him.

I do it because The Light of the World
was extinguished
and no one taught me how to see in the dark.

I do it because my spiritual wisdom
went up in smoke.

I do it because I'm terrified.
I do it in order to be safe.
I do it so I won't have to feel
all this Pain.

I do it because I believe that what this being is offering is love,
and I'm not feeling loved from anyone else at this time.

Nevertheless, the demon accomplished his mission
by helping me sabotage my own.

On this devastating day
I not only lost my father
but I lost my Soul.

I cut my own umbilical cord to Life
and ran away from Home.

And, I wasn't even born yet.

Aftershocks

The days following my father's death
almost led to my death.

As my mother carefully prepared
my father's body for burial,

she helped his soul journey
through the cosmic dimension,

thereby widening the pathway
for all souls
to return to Organic Reality.

All her attention was on him and with him.
And I continued to be left on my own.

I was not fed by food or love,
by that which was human
or divine.

I became malnourished and orphaned.

I didn't know how to ask for what was now missing.
I didn't know if I deserved its return.

My life no longer felt
as valuable as my father,
and I started to die.

The Light at the End

Then my father Returned,

jolting me back to life,
but not to Life.

For the damage had been done,
and could not readily be undone.

Neither my mother
nor I
could touch him.

It was a bittersweet reunion
to be near the one we loved,
but not close enough.

The group, which had scattered
and was bereaved,
rejoined and became revitalized.

But before long
my father left us again,
and this time
for good.

The men in the group took
my father's resurrection
and ran with it,

leaving my mother and me
in the dust.

My Discovery

After my father's resurrection,
my mother started caring for me again,
but she did not resurrect *herself*
as the woman and mother she used to be.

Grief changes signs daily.

Many days, my mother could not
make her body meet the sun.

Other days, she ran about in a frenzy,
desperate and determined
to pick up all the pieces
and put them back together again.

Some days, she raged like a wildfire
against her fate and anyone related to it.

Most days, her sorrow was like a heavy, rolling stone
that flattened every terrain it crossed.

I surfed her feelings with my own,
merging us together,
and then breaking us apart.

It was hard to feel that my presence
wasn't persuading her to heal faster,
and even harder to feel that my presence
might be hampering her healing.

Thankfully, the women ebbed and flowed around her,
sensing when she needed space, a meal, a walk, a hug.

It was during this circling of sisterhood
that my mother's pregnancy became known.
The women rejoiced and drew closer.

The men clapped each other's backs,
certain the pregnancy was a holy sign
and that everything my father didn't complete

I would.

For I was the Son of the Son.

I soaked up this newfangled attention
like fresh blood in a bandage.

The group started pushing and pulling
with their plans for my future.

They did not recognize the leader
who had always stood next to my father,
and my mother at that difficult time
couldn't either.

My mother felt protective of me
but she was vulnerable,
and the restorative hope my presence generated
was a much-needed distraction.

Despite the good news,
none of us nested in safety.

The persecution of our group continued.

Many times I bumped about in terror
as my mother ran for our lives,
one hand steadfastly held under her belly.

When my birth neared,
we moved to what was hoped were safer lands
where I could grow into the man
they needed me to become.

My Birth Day

Nothing ruins a spiritual mission like a vagina.

The shock of my sex shook the group
almost as much as my father's death.

Their crushing disappointment
was the first feeling that greeted me
after I made the strenuous journey
out of my mother's body.

Gasping for breath and blinking against the brightness,
I cried out from under the weight of this cold, new reality
and the heavy expectations that were piled on top of me.

My mother clasped me to her chest,
attempting to shield me
from the group's reaction,

but it was impossible not to feel
the upset happening around me,
because of me.

Then most of the men left.

I moved from the center
of the group's existence
into almost non-existence.

All I knew was that
I was no longer right
for my parents' mission.

My Childhood

I grew into a sensitive,
stubborn,
and solitary child,

who preferred to be with animals
and my handwoven dolls
than other humans.

I spent much of my days
exploring the natural world around me,

studying the elements
and learning their language,

moving my body across the ground
as the sun moved across the sky,

and lying still at night,
gazing at those faraway lights

burning
burning
burning

through darkness.

I rarely followed unnatural rules
or stayed silent
when I witnessed injustice.

My uncommon combination
of blue eyes and dark skin
also raised suspicion and created distance.

One day an older boy stole my beloved doll
who was made out of scraps of red cloth.

Fuming, I sent sparks flying from my hands
igniting a small fire near my bully.

The frightened boy yelped,
threw my doll to the ground,
and bolted away.

As I hugged my salvaged "red lady" to my chest,
I looked toward our hut
and saw my mother cover her laughing mouth.

But later, the boy's parents
and several villagers returned.

What they shouted at us
made my mother's eyes flash
and her cheeks red.

She grabbed me by the arm
and told me I was never to do that again.

I shook loose from her grip,
but not from her worry.

While we roamed safer lands,
we were always looking over our shoulders
and covering our faces.

Fear was a familiar feeling
during my early childhood.

Fear of being found
and fear of being myself.

My Grandmother

The one person I always wanted to find me
was my paternal grandmother,
the only grandparent I knew.

No matter what state I was in,
she would press me into her
warm, round body
that smelled of spices and sweat.

She told me stirring stories of my father when he was a boy,
and I listened, raptly, my heart banging in my chest.

She nourished me with her acceptance,
and I often clung to her strong legs
or watched the world from behind them.

My grandmother was surefooted
and not easily swayed.

Especially not by the men in the group
who clamored for her benedictions and testimony

and yet

never included her wise words
and wider perspective in their tight teachings.

My grandmother had grown
through her grief
into a steady Storm of Grace,

striking with her lightning insights,
shaking with her thunderous knowing,

and leaving all in her path
clearer and livelier.

My grandmother was everything
they feared she was,
and therefore
they tried to contain and control her.

However, if you break
the delicate porcelain
they have encased her in,

She will come back to Life
in you.

And, you will

Experience
the
Uncontrollable
Storm
of
She.

My Studies

A handful of years after I was born,
we traveled to the land of pyramids and sphinxes,
where my mother had me study under
several gifted women in our group.

However, I wasn't much for lessons.
I yearned to play rather than practice,
and I preferred to act from impulse
rather than use techniques.

My lack of discipline and rogue sensibility
amused some of the women and annoyed others.

One time, I was studying under
a high priestess of the psychic arts,
who was healing an ailing woman.

I could sense that the healing
was shallow,
not arising from the depths.

When the priestess turned away,
I instinctually reached out
and touched the suffering woman
with all my heart.

The woman sighed
as her Soul stepped forward
and her pain backed away.

The priestess spun around
and gave me a piercing look,

which I interpreted to mean
I had done something wrong.

Although I yearned to fit in and take part in my parents' community,
I also refused to fit in and take part in my parents' community

for reasons that were mostly hurt feelings
firmly lodged between my lungs.

When the group talked about my father,
they never looked at me.

But I missed him terribly.

I watched other children with their fathers
and experienced a longing *so deep*
it cracked the ground beneath my feet
(which I would then get in trouble for).

And I missed my mother.

For, as her heart was healing,
her role was ripening,
and she was slowly but surely
reclaiming her rightful place.

As I withdrew from the community over the years,
my mother approached the front lines.

She discarded her black robes and donned red.
I discarded my red robes and donned black.

She became an idol,
and I an outcast.

Every time she taught publicly,
I only felt our differences.

Now it was even clearer,
for all to see.

What she and my father were,
I was not
and would never be.

The Turn

Although some men in the group revered my mother,
many felt threatened by and envious of
how she understood my father's mission
better than they did . . .

and how she *completed it.*

For she is the Omega to his Alpha.

My father's teachings of nonviolence,
humility, and love for all,

contrasted sharply with the opinions
of the oppressed crowds around us
and the loud battle cries within them.

If my mother continued to teach
and expand my father's message,

many men felt certain they would lose
what little respect and followers
they had worked so hard to gain.

One man who hovered heavily
around my father while he was alive
openly despised my mother.

He incited some into such an impassioned frenzy
that plans were made to end my mother's life
and my own.

[pause]

This might sound conspiratorial,
even incomprehensible.

But all I am doing is sharing my experience.

Thankfully, a few loyal men and women
became aware of the plans
and took action.

A politician and philosopher,
who had always been kind to us
and was the closest thing I ever had to a father,
arranged for our safe passage.

To my young heart's dismay,
he stayed behind in order to
distract and derail
those searching for us.

Under the cover of a new moon
a small group of us,
including my grandmother,

left these loaded lands and sailed north
toward my mother's land of origin.

A Safer Passage

Our voyage across the sea
made me physically sick,
and heartsick.

For my grandmother was called
to a land we weren't.

With tears pouring down my face,
I begged my mother to let me stay
with my grandmother,

but they both agreed
that my place
was somewhere else.

As I hugged my only consistent source
of comfort goodbye, she whispered:

"Trust yourself, Sarah.
And learn to Love yourself."

Instructions that I am only now beginning to follow.

Our small group sailed on
till my mother said,
"Here."

As we approached the coast
that would become our new home,
a group was present to greet us.

As my feet touched this new land,
I felt relief.

As my eyes met these new eyes,
I felt accepted.

For the warm-hearted people
who greeted us
were dark-skinned outcasts
like me.

My mother smiled at me
as I experienced their welcome.

And I tentatively smiled back.

Home Making

My mother taught and traveled
throughout this new land.

Exploring the fecund marsh,
floating in the frothy sea,
and riding the wild, white horses
filled her absence.

As did my new friends.

I spent much time
listening to their stories,
dancing to their music,
and gazing into their fires.

They too, came from a far-away land,
seeking shelter and a new life.

But due to the color of their skin
and the colorful practices of their tribes,
they were treated unfairly
by the pale-skinned, cool-bodied locals.

I began to stand for my friends
when they were beaten down,

speak for them
when they were silenced,

and fight for their right
to live in peace.

For the first time
since I left the womb,
I felt like I had a mission.

The Touch

While I was finding redemption
in my new vocation
my mother was expanding her own

into heated territories that many,
including myself back then,
misunderstood.

While she taught about True Love
to all who asked for it,

she also began Touching *as* Love
with a few who were ready for it.

I found this out the hard way.

Late one night,
as I rode through the countryside
under a bright moon,

I happened upon a private ritual
involving my mother
and a man I didn't know.

She was doing something I thought she only did with my father.
Something I believed she *should* only do with my father.

I was shocked.
Her disloyalty burned a hole
in my stomach.

I didn't tell my mother I saw her,
but after that night
I lashed out at her to such an extent
that she traveled farther and farther away.

Until there was enough distance between us
to sufficiently disconnect me from my early life.

And then
it was just me
and my horses

and a cause I fervidly fought for
to cover my pain.

My Original Role

Years passed, and I developed
a respectable presence in the land
that had nothing to do with my parents
or former community.

I was proud of my modest accomplishments
and my simple life of service.

Then I received a message that my mother was dying,
and my self-created world imploded.

I rode to her cave as quickly as I could
and collapsed by her side in grief.

She looked at me with nothing
but Love and Understanding.

She looked at me the way
she had *always* looked at me,
but I could only recognize,
and receive,
now.

Everything was forgiven.

Everything I had placed
between us
now
drew us closer.

But, not close enough.

Because my mother made a strange request.

She asked if she could hold me,
like she didn't do enough
when I was a child.

I tearfully complied,
crawled into her lap,
and let myself

Be
Held

by Her . . .

and then
also

by Him.

I felt as I once did in the womb,
and before the womb.

Our three hearts beating together

In True Love's Embrace,
my Mother
and
my Father

Reminded
me
of my
Original Role.

And
I accepted
It.

A Different Leader

Although I accepted my role,
not everyone accepted me.

There was no denying that
I was different than my parents.

And very different than what the people
who had never met my parents
believed (and wanted) my parents to be.

But, my parents left a prominent impression
to encourage us to leave our own.

My parents did not want us to imitate,
they wanted us to originate.

They invited us to be like every other
living organism on the earth
and simply

Be Ourselves.

Nothing more
and nothing less.

While I knew and spoke these Natural Truths,
I did not live them at the time.

I felt plagued by unworthiness
and the primal need to prove myself

in order to win the never-before-given
acceptance from my parents' group.

Still,
stories of my parents'
once lost,
but now found,
daughter
spread.

My Teaching

Although I had watched my mother teach countless times,
I was unprepared for the outbreak of terror
that strangled my voice and shook me out of my skin
during my first public gathering.

Nevertheless,

I
fell
into place
as
the Third.

Afterward, people swarmed,
asking questions, sharing realizations,
and giving thanks.

One man watching me closely
looked and felt eerily familiar.
Rage radiated off his body.

He followed the group back to our dwellings
and attended our community meal,

all the while
staring at me

like he was seeing a ghost.

When I asked who he was,
the women told me
he had been close to my father
and zealously preached his message.

This made me curious and wary,
but by the end of the night
his foreboding demeanor had shifted
into something friendlier,
and he made his way next to me.

He told me that because he was one
of only a few in this land
who had known *both*
my father and my mother,

he could help me become the daughter
they always wanted me to be.

I just needed to root out
Something inside me

that was poisoning
my parents' teachings,

and could harm others
and cause others to harm me.

My body froze
and my heart broke

as my worst fear
about myself
was affirmed.

I found myself shrinking
in front of this older, wiser, spiritual man
and I heard a frightened, fetal part of me
cry out for his help.

He nodded with approval
and told me he would send men to fetch me
the day after morrow.

As he got up to leave,
he leaned down and whispered
that it would be best
if we kept our plans secret.

I nodded numbly
and hung my head in shame
that I had such a Thing inside me.

Such a Thing that could ruin everything
my parents lived and died for.

The Betrayal

My escorts arrived in the middle of the night.
Two of the men had guarded my mother and me
when I was young, which settled my churning stomach.

We traveled discreetly, eventually reaching a cavern
where we took a boat to my new residence.

The man was there to greet us.

As he helped me out of the boat,
he tossed a sack of coins to the guards
who hastily rowed away.

I was led down a ladder
to an underground chamber
equipped with everything I would need,
except sunlight.

For an unknown time,
the man stayed with me in that dark room,
only leaving me for bodily needs and sleep.

It felt like an initiation,
and not unlike what I had experienced
as a child during my failed studies.

The man asked me to share what I had learned

from my mother,
from my father,
from myself.

So, I did.

Sometimes tears filled his eyes as I spoke.
Sometimes we held hands in awed silence.

Sometimes the storm clouds cleared from his heart,
and he really and truly Saw me . . .
and didn't look away.

For the first time in my life,
I didn't feel so alone.

I had a confidant,
and what began to feel like
a genuine friend.

Like a dam breaking,
I poured *everything* out,
and he received it all.

But after some time,
he began to correct me.

Patiently explaining where and how I was wrong
regarding my own and my parents' teachings.

The man's desire
to carry out my father's mission
was potent,

and my desire
to deserve my new role
was dominant.

I grew more and more confused
as his strong convictions muted my memories,
and I began to doubt myself.

The man started to point out
whenever that Something
in me arose.

The Thing that poisoned my parents' teachings.
The Thing that could get me, and those close to me, killed.

One time, when this Thing was active,
the man had me describe
what this Thing looked and felt like,
which happened to be one in the same.

This poisonous and dangerous
Thing
in me,
was

Red.

This identification alarmed my friend.

Our practices grew more extreme,
most of which involved exorcising

Red

from my body
and my parents' teachings.

After a while
I was physically weak,
emotionally drained,
mentally disoriented,
and *Soulless.*

I was exactly how he wanted me.

This man, who was close to my father,
and who I thought was my friend,
entered my chamber one day

and told me I had given him everything he needed
and now he was giving me everything I deserved.

He climbed out of my underground cell,
rolled a large rock on top of my exit,

and built *his* church on top of it.

Burying me,
in the dark.

Until now.

The Present

Childhood

I was born in Atlanta, Georgia,
to loving Catholic parents
who named me Sarah.

I was a strong-willed, inquisitive,
and sensitive child
who talked to animals, trees,
and our family's station wagon.

And God.

In fact, I was *in love* with God
and wanted to be a priest when I grew up
but learned that wasn't an option
because I was a girl.

I was terrified of being locked in the basement
(something my mischievous sisters took full advantage of),

went through a phase where I graffitied
my name on every wall around me
(it felt necessary to leave my mark),

and an even longer phase
where I was convinced
that I was adopted.

Even while surrounded
by a wonderful family,
I felt like an orphan.

But all in all, I had a fortunate, healthy,
stable, and relatively happy childhood.

When I was in sixth grade, I read
a book about reincarnation.

The Reality of us Returning
again and again
in order to learn and grow as souls,

seemed as natural as the continuous,
yet always-changing seasons,

exceptionally compassionate
(to have more than one chance at life),

and honestly, sort of *duh.*

The local priest didn't think so.

Even after I prattled about how many
early Christians believed in reincarnation.
(Did I mention that I was a *wee* bit of a spiritual smart ass?)

He shooed me out of the confessional booth
hauling a heavy bucket of penance,
which I dumped
as I walked out of the Church
for good.

My open-minded parents respected my departure
from our family's religion
but emphasized how important it was that I find

Something

I believed in.

Magical Mystery Tour

That was all the permission I needed
to spend the next few decades of my life
on a magical mystery tour of the Universe.

I read every spiritual book I could get my eager hands on,
visited every holy person who floated through town,
had my chakras aligned, my aura cleansed, my stars read,
and for numerological reasons
changed the spelling of my name from "Sarah" to "Sera."

To ground my obsession with all things spiritual,
I rigorously studied world religions in college and graduate school
and traveled around the world investigating their lived reality.

I moved to San Francisco after graduate school
and submerged myself in the Northern California whirlpool
of spiritual and self-help movements.

After a few years in San Francisco, I wrote and published *The Red Book:
A Deliciously Unorthodox Approach to Igniting Your Divine Spark,*
which was aimed at young women who I felt had been left out of spirituality.

However, the magnitude of fear and panic
that coursed through my body
when I presented my work publicly
made "stage fright" feel more like "stage death."

Something else started to happen at this time in my life:
spine-curling bouts of pain during some of my periods.

Every episode happened late at night,
foreshadowed by a dream where I was
viciously attacked by a demon I could not see.

Not exactly something my gynecologist
could write a prescription for.

To try and help ease and better understand
my agonizing physical reactions
to my budding spiritual career,

I found an esoteric school in California
where recalling past lives was as common
as recalling childhood memories,
and dealing with interfering forces was as ordinary
as dealing with invasive neighbors.

Although remembering previous lives
when I was tortured or killed for speaking my truth publicly
explained *some* of my reactions to my career,
and although learning to protect myself from interfering forces
provided temporary relief,

my body did not heal,
my terror of going public did not lessen,
and the interference only increased.

I left the esoteric school after a year.

The embarrassing truth was
despite my vast and varied spiritual studies,
travels, and experiences,

I could not find a tradition, lineage, community,
school, practice, trend, or even a teacher
that *really* resonated with my heart.

Red Winks

Now it's not that *nothing*
in my spiritual explorations
resonated with me.

Something

had repeatedly poked me
in the chest over the years,
and that Something

showed
up
as

Red.

Kali, the fierce Hindu Goddess of destruction and creation,
awakened dark, tight, hidden parts of me
with Her long, red tongue.

Eve whispered in my left ear
the Real Reason why
she tasted that red apple:
to Know Herself.

Lilith welcomed me to dance ecstatically
with her on the shores of the Red Sea.

The Whore of Babylon raised her cup of red wine
and toasted my bloody female body,

my natural sensuality,
and my divine right to experience pleasure.

Female mystics from every spiritual tradition
reminded me that we have only been taught
half of the divine's story
—the masculine half—
and therefore only half of *our* story.

And then there were my dreams.

Where I was running, running, running
with a tiny fetus in the palm of my hand,
desperate to save its life.

At some point in the dream
the fetus would fly toward a couple making love
under a luminous Red Light.

The couple was Jesus and Magdalene.

The Red winks amped up in my late twenties,
flirting through songs on the radio,
movies, billboards, roses, wine.

Everywhere I looked,

Red
Looked
Back.

It felt like I was being wooed
by Something Specific and Sacred,
and it made me giddy and grateful.

I started to call this strangely familiar Presence
that winked through these Red mediums
the Red Lady.

We began to commune
like Close Friends.

Our Love grew like a wild fire.

A wild fire I let
BLAZE
in my personal life.

However.

Nobody knew *Who* I was referring to
when I talked about
the Red Lady this and the Red Lady that.

Neither did I.

It didn't help that She was a *She*
and that She was Red.

As we know, the Feminine has been exiled
from almost every religion,
and Red isn't often viewed as a very "spiritual" color,
and through some lenses,
Red symbolizes rage, our base nature, sexuality, and evil.

So, over the years, I developed a painful habit.

When my Red Lady clashed
with the spiritual realities I was exploring,
I abandoned Her.

My spiritual pride, self-doubt,
and fears of being seen as woo-woo
or undeveloped, delusional, or wrong
often overruled my authentic experiences of Her.

If spiritual traditions didn't know the Red Lady,
maybe She didn't actually exist.

The Shake Down

In 2009, I signed a large contract for my second book,
was interviewed and featured in the *New York Times*,
and received several promising and lucrative offers.

I felt like I was on mission.

But then my life fell apart
when I met the Jungian psychoanalyst
Marion Woodman.

The difference between us
was a titanic transmission.

She was full of Herself.

She knew her soul, *intimately.*
It filled her entire body.

She radiated,
not with spiritual light,
but with soulful realness.

She was Here.
She was All In.

I abruptly woke up to the fact
that despite my spiritual knowledge and mystical experiences,
my booming social life and successful career,
I was *not* ensouled.

In fact, I could not find
my soul
at all.

Like a sheet ripped off an empty bed,
I suddenly realized that most of me
was missing.

Although I looked and acted the part,
I wasn't Human.

Although I had a pulse,
I wasn't Alive.

Although I had a body,
I wasn't Incarnate.

Although I passionately (and publicly) preached the opposite,
the truth was that I was gravely disconnected
from my humanity, my feelings, my flesh, my primal needs,
intimate relationships, other humans, and the earth Herself.

And I had been living
in this soulless, disembodied way
for all of my life.

The shock and pain of this recognition
humbled me and completely mystified me.

When I inquired about why and how I had lost my soul,
trauma shook my body, core wounds opened,
and darker-than-dark feelings surfaced:

I *hated* being human (and other humans).
I was terrified of being in a body and living on this earth.
In fact, I would rather be dead than alive.

The extreme nature of my newly disclosed
feelings and trauma
stunned me, surprised my therapists,
and befuddled highly regarded trauma specialists.

For we could not locate the roots
in this life.

The Red Tent

To help find my missing soul,
I pulled away from my professional and social life
and created a physical and spiritual cocoon
that I called the Red tent.

A lot happened during my three years in the Red tent,
(much of which I share in my second book,
Red Hot and Holy, which I wrote while in the tent)

and included

intensive psychological work (I was dissociative and avoidant),
extensive career changes (from mainstream success to my soul's kind of success),
and spiritual redirection (from transcendence to immanence).

I was a spiritual bypasser
who (unconsciously) used spirituality
like one uses a drug

—as a *defense* against the harsh realities of life,
the human condition
and the soul.

In the Red tent, I began to detox.

I gave away all my spiritual books
and stopped going to workshops,
listening to teachers, and using practices.

I discarded my spiritual studies and beliefs
and began to nurture my natural impulses
and rebuild trust in my inner knowing.

Slowly but surely
I started to find my way through
the cosmic dimension.

Throughout this process,
I inquired who the Red Lady was
but never found an answer.

The mystifying mind-fuck was that my Red Lady
felt as infinite and essential to me as the Creatrix
and had Divinely Feminine qualities,
but my Red Lady also felt *different* than the Creatrix.

At one point, frustrated and worried that Red
was a cosmic distraction
or a sly symptom of spiritual bypassing,
I pushed Red far away from me.

About six months later, my then-publisher
refused to publish my "strange" book manuscript
(the one I had written while in the Red tent),

and my then-best friend received a publishing deal
and came out in the world with *her* own work about red.

It was the perfect set
of external circumstances and internal collisions
to puncture my core wounds,
deep enough

that
Red
gushed out,

making me Remember and Realize
in every cell of my female body,
that Red was *my eternal Divine Soul,*

whom I had distrusted and given away
not just in this life, but in all of my lives.

Remembering myself as a sovereign Divine Soul
who was a visiting fractal from another Universe
felt like the pinnacle of my journey.

Although I knew it would be a lifelong endeavor,
I believed I had reached my final step:
embodying my Divine Soul.

But I was wrong,
sort of.

Turns out, the Real Way
to embody my divinity
is through my humanity.

Put differently: I can't embody my Divine Soul
without embodying my human soul.

Sarah's Reveal

I became aware of Sarah while I was in the Red tent.
However, the importance isn't *how* Sarah revealed herself,
it's how I felt when she first did:

I felt Found.

The focal piece of my puzzle
was put in its place
by a Hand bigger than my own,
and my Whole Picture
snapped into view.

In those initial suspended moments,

I didn't just Remember
an essential piece
of my soul,

I also Understood
why I am the way I am
as a human.

A Truth trailing behind all my truths
tackled me to the ground that day
and would not let me stand back up without It . . .

without Sarah.

Swallowing Sarah

Needless to say, Sarah is a big red pill to swallow
and way too easy to spit out.

For it is one thing to know and embrace your Divine Soul.
It's another thing to know and embrace your human soul.

And it's something else altogether
when a fragmented piece of your human soul
that is seeking integration
identifies herself as Jesus Christ and Mary Magdalene's
abandoned love child.

Especially if you are a critically minded, psychologically reflexive,
energetically astute, spiritually rigorous modern woman
who went to Harvard.

I've explored many possibilities,
starting with the obvious:

A previously unconscious part of me is using
the symbol, metaphor, story, and possible reality
of Jesus and Magdalene's lost daughter
in order to process trauma and heal my wounds.

I *am* a middle child and a "4" in the Enneagram,
which means that when I'm out of balance or living unconsciously
I crave attention, desire to feel special, and have a flair for drama.
All of which are also fitting characteristics for someone with "Sarah's wounds."

I've considered that many, if not all, women
suffer from "Sarah's wounds"
and feel (or have felt) dismissed,

silenced, and at times
like their soul has been "buried alive."

If we widen the lens even more,
we could theorize that Sarah
is not just a missing piece of *my* soul,
but of *all* of our souls
(women, men, and those in between),

which would make each of us
part of a larger archetypal process
of "Remembering and Reclaiming Sarah."

Other possibilities I've explored are that Sarah is a:

delusion, sub-personality, complex (messianic, most likely), PTSD,
shadow, projection, inner child, imaginary friend, active imagination therapy,
part of the collective unconscious, ancestor, genetic memory,
lineage link, karmic agreement, New Age fantasy, childish fairy tale,
walk in, lost soul (but not mine), descended master, spirit guide, nefarious being,
energetic overlay, cosmic counterfeit, metaphysical manipulation, etc.

I'm relatively confident that anything
you might wonder or suppose about
who and what Sarah is,
I have wondered and investigated, too.

But here's something I've learned the hard way:

While it's crucial to question and doubt
all "beings" that stake a claim in us,
it's cruel to torture them.

In other words, if we're not careful,
our intellectual, spiritual, and psychological
credentials and acumen

can kill that which is genuinely trying
to come back to Life in us.

At the beginning of our conscious relationship,
Sarah was like a skittish, starving, feral animal
who had been kept in isolation for way too long
and did not know how to trust the only hand that could feed her.

Sarah had good reason to distrust me
and doubt my ability to care for her
because I had never cared for my soul before.

Soul Fragments

Despite my doubts and intellectual bullying of Sarah,
which arose soon after she revealed herself,
she was not easy to shake.

Everywhere I looked,
an All-Knowing finger pointed
not at me, but through me,
at *Sarah*.

After my encounter with Marion Woodman,
I had become fairly proficient
at recognizing and retrieving soul fragments.

Here's how this normally goes down:

Something will (or will not) happen in my life,
and I will start to feel a "tug" from a displaced part of me
that is significantly different in feeling than
a purely psychological force, such as a complex or "part."

After identifying that I am indeed dealing with a soul fragment,
I will quiet my mind, sink into my body,
and start to inquire about how this soul loss happened.

Soon enough, I will start to remember
something that happened recently
or in early childhood
or in another life
or on a different dimension.

Sometimes my soul will fragment due to shock, trauma, or pain
from the loss of a loved one, an accident, a crisis of faith,
abuse, a natural disaster, or any threatening event.

Sometimes the soul loss is because of something *I* have done
such as staying too long in an unhealthy relationship;
not speaking up when I needed to;
or putting my career, money, social standards, opinions of others
—or a spiritual teacher, paradigm, or practice—in front of my soul.

Sometimes part of my soul sneaks away
due to something as seemingly small as
a parent or friend getting upset with me,
a grade-school teacher calling out my mistakes,
a stranger looking at me the wrong way,
or watching the nightly news.

Often my soul will fragment because
I can't handle feeling
what I am feeling at that time.

After I remember when and why my soul fragmented,
I locate and connect with the piece,
kind of like a TV picks up a satellite signal.

Most soul fragments are stuck in a reality
they believe is real.

They keep replaying the scene
where they fragmented
over and over again.

Locating these soul pieces,
letting them express their reality,
and then helping them realize
that while their feelings are real
their reality isn't,

is part of, but not all of,
what is needed
for them to come home.

For the more traumatized pieces,
outside help from a trained professional
is often necessary.

However, inside help is *always* available.

Our Divine Soul not only knows
the ins and outs of our human psyche,
It knows the ins and outs of our
entire incarnational and Universal journey.

This is because our human soul
is the part of our Divine Soul
that is here on Earth.

Therefore, our Divine Soul knows
how far and wide It has cast Itself,
what it takes to reel Itself back in,
and importantly, *when* to do so.

Trusting our organic timeline
and our body's and Soul's subtle guidance
is how we stay healthy, safe, and on *our* path.

However, I was stumbling down
an unpaved path.

Sarah was unlike any soul fragment
I had ever encountered before.

Sarah's Fragments

Sarah came at me with a knife
between her teeth,
dirt beneath her ripped nails,
and a savage look in her eyes.

Her words carried the force
of two thousand years
of suppression and silence
—as did her feelings.

She was enraged and embittered,
soaked in shame and self-loathing,
bristling with pride, and brimming with blame.

In other words, she showed up as she had been left behind.

And as if every second since her first human life
had twisted her into a tighter knot.

Sarah was as complicated as any human,
and what was even more fascinating
was that Sarah had soul fragments

stuck in traumatic and painful events of her life,
specifically her father's crucifixion,
her birth, and her death.

Therefore, I was not only retrieving a supposed soul fragment,
I was also busy retrieving a supposed soul fragment's soul fragments.

Almost every day, through something that was happening in my own life,
I was encouraged to remember a related part of Sarah's story,
locate another (or the same) piece of her soul,
let her express herself,
and then try to share a broader and healthier perspective with her.

It was time-consuming, demanding, and grueling.

But it also felt like the most important
and necessary inner work
I had ever done.

Fetus Sarah

The most influential and multifaceted fragment of Sarah
was her fetus fragment,
the part of Sarah that split during the crucifixion.

There was *so* much trauma, terror, and pain
enveloping the fetus
that initially I didn't know what to do for her.

I felt Sarah's trauma in my own womb.

I often placed my hands on my locked pelvis
while working with her, attempting to reground us
and relieve both of our pain.

But fetus Sarah refused to inhabit
her body and this earth.

She was locked shut against Life.

And I couldn't help but feel
how much I was, as well.

When I worked with the aspect of fetus Sarah
who sold her Soul to the demon,

I recognized my own lack of proper boundaries
and inability to discern healthy relationships.

I also identified a previously unconscious belief
that I will only be safe and loved
if I give away my troublesome Soul and mission.

The bitter truth was that I sold out my Soul on a regular basis.

Newborn Sarah

The next fragment I was repeatedly pulled toward was newborn Sarah,
the part of Sarah that fragmented right after she was born
due to feeling rejected by her first community.

This fragment of newborn Sarah felt unwanted
and unable to participate in her parents' mission
because something was wrong with her.

She believed that she would never be nourished
by human relationships or get her essential needs met.

Working with newborn Sarah, I recognized
how much I distrust
and struggle to bond with others.

And how I've been afraid to identify and voice my needs
from fear of rejection
or from having to admit how they are *not* being met
by those close to me and, most importantly, by myself.

I also acknowledged that lurking underneath my own work in the world
was a fierce need to be accepted and finally prove myself,
underscored by a relentless fear that I would disappointment everyone.

Perhaps behind my spiritual vocation and passion to be of service
was a broken soul's agenda to be wanted and loved.

Child and Teenage Sarah

Child Sarah darted away from me
every chance she could.

She felt neglected by her mother,
ignored by her spiritual community,
and different than other children around her.

But she was just fine on her own
and could take care of herself
thank you very much!

That lone-wolf,
refusal-to-ask-for-help attitude
is one I could relate to.

Connecting with child Sarah helped me admit
how different from others and lonely I feel,
and how much I yearn for, yet avoid, community.

Interacting with teenage Sarah
was like interacting with a middle finger.

One phrase best describes her attitude
toward me, you, her parents, her community,
and all spiritual authorities:

Fuck
you.

I have always had to hold down my "middle finger,"
which wants to raise at just about every spiritual authority
or religious institution in existence, *especially* the Church.

I thought it was just because I was a freedom-loving rebel
who was told as a child I couldn't be a priest,
and who now takes a heretic's delight in "sticking it to the man."

Maybe it's also because I've had
a supremely pissed-off spiritually ostracized teenager
trapped inside me for two thousand years.

Adult Sarah

Working with adult Sarah was like
working in the pitch-black dark.

She had been buried underground for so long
that she was an empty shell
—pale, skeletal, and starved of Life.

When I first found her, she could barely register me.

She had given up on ever being found.
She also didn't *want* to be found.

She believed she was an epic failure,
and felt unworthy of Life or Love.

When I approached her, no matter how softly,
she vehemently turned away from me
toward the desolate darkness behind her.

[deep breath]

Though I visited Sarah frequently
and our relationship grew stronger and healthier,

Sarah's three main fragments
—the fetus, newborn, and dying adult—
refused to come home with me
for reasons I could not figure out.

I quickly learned that I could not force
Sarah to do anything,
nor could I control this process.

I also experienced that it's downright abusive
to feed a fragmented soul spiritual platitudes like:

"There is no past or future; there is only now."
"Just *let it go*."
"Don't get stuck in your story."
"Focus on the light and stay positive."

Soul work necessitates that we stick to our story
or stay in the dark or sink under water
for as fucking long as we need to.

Soul Work

Working with Sarah was confronting,
to say the least.

Though foreign in shape and story,
Sarah was more than familiar
in feelings and energy.

She had been kicking and screaming,
or silent and steaming,
underneath every aspect of my life,

including every relationship I had entered (and exited),
each book I had written,
not to mention all my health conditions
and spiritual ambitions.

Sarah had been hiding in plain sight.

On one occasion, when I was struggling
with immense feelings of guilt and loss
around leaving town for a few months
without my intimate partner
in order to write this book,

our couple's therapist asked me:
"Who did that in your life?
Who left you to pursue their path?"

I could make plenty of sensible mental associations
for why I was feeling the way I was,
like because I was weaned from my mother,
or because my dad traveled a lot for work when I was a child.

Or because some of my friends were so focused
on their personal transformation
that they didn't focus as much on our human connection.
(I did live in Northern California for eleven years.)

Or maybe I feared abandoning an aspect of myself,
like my femininity,
by pursuing my spiritual path
—a traditionally masculine endeavor.

And so on and so forth.

But later that night, while taking a shower,
I doubled over
as another truth washed over my body,
as tangible as the hot water itself.

Sarah's parents left her to pursue their spiritual mission!
And I'm desperately trying not to do the same thing to someone I love.

While Sarah's feelings are undeniably universal,
they also felt like the intensely personal feelings
of a tormented girl from two thousand years ago,
which resulted from her particular life experiences.

They also felt like the feelings that had erupted
out of me
after my meeting with Marion Woodman.

Although I tried not to take detours from my life,
crossovers happened so often
that I wished I could take *Sarah* to therapy.

But I didn't.

Because how the hell was I supposed to share this
and *not* be diagnosed as delusional
or suffering from a host of other pathologies.

Yet, what became difficult to deny
was that whenever I went back to "Sarah's life,"
something almost always shifted in my life.

For example, when Sarah first revealed herself
I was suffering through a year-long writer's block
around my second book.

I tried many different things to help break my block
—therapy, writing exercises, self-help practices, coaches, shamans,
psychics, silent retreats, expressive arts, flower essences—
but nothing had worked.

The day after working with Sarah's resistance to *her* life's work,
my writer's block broke,
and I was then able to complete *Red Hot and Holy.*

It wasn't always this dramatic,
but it was frequently noticeable.

My work with Sarah was (and still is) therapeutic,
but as months turned into years

it became harder for me to believe that Sarah was a delusion
or just a psychological exercise like active imagination
or only an archetype, symbol, metaphor
or fantastical person from the past
who I was projecting upon in order to heal.

I had to admit to myself what I was terrified to admit
from the moment I first became aware of her:

Sarah felt as real as I did.

Cosmic Cobwebs

Before we move on, I want to clear away
a few cosmic cobwebs.

I do not receive "visitations" from Sarah
or experience visions of her.

This is *not* a psychic seeing.
This is a human remembering.

Until our reunion, which you will read about later,
I experienced Sarah as a being separate from me,
and I simultaneously felt myself *as* that separated being.

My memories are not *of* Sarah,
but rather, *from* Sarah.

Put differently: information about Sarah
does not come from an external source,
nor is it "presented" to me,
nor are my memories "inserted" into me.

I mention this because *synthetic* memories
and the resulting, often intense, simulated emotions
are a common cosmic phenomenon and trickery,
and *one* of the reasons why people believe they are
reincarnations of someone "important" in the past.

This spiritual subterfuge works because we humans
long to feel special and like our existence *matters*.

Plus we have shadows; covert ambitions; repressed desires for power;
and myriad unconscious parts, wounds, and needy aspects of ourselves
—including sincere yearnings to be of service.

Rigorous psychological and shadow work,
vigilant energetic boundaries and discernment,
and ongoing multidimensional self-inquiry

are a must for those of us who get tapped
on the shoulder by a possible "past incarnation,"
especially if it claims to be someone
"significant" from the past.

Remember: Feel for the Real.
Feel for that which can't be faked or forged.

If your experiences are shiny and showy
like you're visiting a multidimensional multiplex,
or if they feel overpowering, disembodied, or *cosmic*,
you've probably bypassed the soul realm.

The soul realm is subtle, grounding, sobering.
It brings you down and in, not up and out.

Soul memories are somewhat muted,
like recalling a tune you haven't heard for decades.

Soul memories are familiar,
manifest from and in your body,
and should be directly related to,
and reflected in, your ordinary life.

A soul fragment should feel like a part of you.
Often a painful, shameful, traumatized, or unacceptable part of you
for those are common reasons why it isn't integrated.

To be blunt:

I am not using Sarah for a career boost
or to set myself up as the next Big Thing.

However, I fully realize and admit
that sharing my experiences of Sarah
as part of my own soul
can appear as though I am claiming
to be someone "special."

But the more I sit in this precarious position
the more I realize that that's partly because
most people don't know Sarah's story.

And because of the cosmic falsifications, religious distortions,
and spiritual projections that smother Jesus and Magdalene
and, really, most prominent spiritual figures from the past.

It's tough to acknowledge the mundane and messy *humanity*
of spiritual teachers, leaders, and sages like Jesus and Magdalene
and the equally powerful and uniquely special *divinity*
that exists within ourselves.

Nor is my work with Sarah about searching for secret teachings,
uncovering conspiracies, corralling (and correcting) historical facts,
scavenging archeological sites, scrutinizing ancient texts, debating theology,
starting a new religion, or harboring elitist mystical knowledge.

What I share in "The Past"
about Jesus and Magdalene
and Life and Love,

Every Body Knows.

My work with Sarah
is about embodying my soul

so I can be a better human
and bring a bit more
Love and Life to this planet.

The Unreal Reality of Sarah

When I was with Sarah and my Parents
in the soul realm,
nothing felt more Real.

But, when I re-entered
the loud dominance
of everyday reality,

my intimate connection
with Sarah and my Parents
often felt unreal.

My rational mind
and the collective consciousness
beat my Redvelations to a pulp.

However, this Universe is extremely persistent
and our souls, quite determined.

Often a sign or synchronicity
would brush across my life in such a way that
my doubts and disbelief would diffuse . . .
temporarily.

A few small, but sweet, examples:

Soon after Sarah revealed herself,
the supposed tibia bone of Mary Magdalene
left its sacred nook in Europe for the first time ever
and went on a world tour,

which happened to stop
in my hometown,
exactly on my birthday.

When I approached the glass-encased
ancient bone
and laid a red rose at its base,

every part of me was embraced
by nothing other
than my Mother's Love.

One agonizing morning a few years after Sarah's reveal,
I felt like I was making zero progress
and that Sarah would be stuck forever in her painful past.

On our afternoon walk, my dogs pulled me toward
a booming (and hot-dog grilling) graduation party
with a bright-red sign flapping in the wind that read:

"The Future Is Yours, Sarah!"

[pause]

Although I might wow you (or not)
by sharing hundreds of signs and synchronicities
related to Sarah,

I don't want to have to prove to you
Something that is Real for me.

More important than the signs and synchronicities
are the feelings that accompany them.

Feelings that relay far more Truth and Love
and gut-punching honesty

than all my doubts, thoughts, and theories
about this baffling soul work.

And so that's what I began to trust:
my feelings.

Ironically, I often avoided Sarah
because of *her* feelings.

The Runaway

Though I consciously accepted this surreal soul work
I was doing with Sarah,
unconsciously I tried to run away from it.

But I couldn't run away for too long
without Sarah tripping me up.

A few years after I became aware of Sarah,
I was preparing a talk for a women's conference
when I was struck by severe and debilitating migraines,
which were uncommon occurrences for me.

A gifted and highly trained woman
did a shamanic journey
to try to locate the cause of my pain.

She called me after the journey, her voice hesitant:

"Sera, in the journey I just did for you regarding the root of your migraines,
I saw a pregnant woman running for her life and the life of her baby."

[pause]

"The woman was Mary Magdalene."

I shook my aching noggin.

I had avoided checking in with Sarah while writing the talk
and so now she was checking into my head.

I immediately got off the phone,
zoomed in on Sarah,
and found her to be *freaking* out.

She did *not* want me including
an incendiary part about Jesus in my talk.
She was terrified of me being publicly linked to him
and felt certain I was putting my life in danger.

It took a lot of personal coaching to get Sarah
to stop banging on my poor head
and to get us on board a flight to Denver,

where I was able to deliver the talk without being killed,
which helped Sarah trust me and my public work
a *little* more.

Unfortunately, I have many stories like this one.

When I didn't take Sarah into account,
I was reminded in some gentle or rough way

that whether I liked it or not,
understood it or not,
or even agreed with it or not,

Sarah and I were intrinsically tied together.

But my, oh my, am I a resistant one.

Sarah's Work

For years, Sarah was my secret.

While a few close friends knew about her,
I kept Sarah behind the red-velvet curtains
of my public life.

However, it became clear
while writing *Red Hot and Holy*
that I needed to include Sarah
because she was intimately related to the Red Lady
whom the entire book was devoted to.

The fear of sharing Sarah publicly
was beyond anything I had experienced
thus far.

So, I was meticulous.

I only shared small, digestible bites
of our relationship in *Red Hot and Holy*,
carefully guarding against what could cause others to reject us,
focusing on the more archetypal elements of Sarah
that we all share.

One year after *Red Hot and Holy* was published,
I was invited to facilitate a private retreat.

As the date of the retreat approached,
the man who invited me sent me a thoughtful email
informing me that I did not have to hold anything back
and I was welcome to do my Soul's Work
with his open-hearted community.

Usually I overplanned, micromanaged, and white-knuckled it
through every minute of my public events
due to my staggering stage fright.

I desperately wanted to do my "Soul's Work"
at these events, but I didn't entirely know what it was.

So after I read this man's email, I panicked.

My fears of failing at what was being asked of me
were so convincing that it took all I had
not to write the man back and cancel the event.

My overblown reaction to his unassuming invitation
was a clue that something deeper was going on,
so I ventured into the soul realm.

I found myself in what had unfortunately come to be a familiar scene:
when Sarah gave her Divine Soul to the demon during the crucifixion.

I suddenly understood that doing what this man was inviting
me to do didn't just feel intimidating for the usual reasons,
it also felt *impossible.*

For how could Sarah or Sera
do her Soul's Work in the world
without her Soul?

But then I felt my Red Lady's Loving Presence,
and I gained Her Bigger Perspective.

I Realized that no matter
what it appeared like or felt like,
what was *actually* impossible

was Sarah ever separating
from her Divine Soul
in the first place.

It was a sinister sleight of hand, a devious illusion
that the demon did everything he could to perpetuate.

The image in the soul realm was of Sarah
staring at a blank wall, bawling her eyes out,
not seeing that what was behind the thin wall
and surrounding her, thickly, on all sides

was her Red Lady,
her Infinite Divine Soul

that *never* goes away
no matter what she does
or doesn't do.

Now, with the help from her "outside eyes"
—myself and our Lady—
Sarah's walled reality ceased being her only reality.

Sarah stopped weeping.
She slowly walked toward the fake wall
and, using barely any force,
pushed it,
causing it to fall back in a cloud of dust.

The always-present Red Light it had previously blocked
shone brightly on her awestruck face.

And, just like that, the spell broke.

I opened my eyes.
My mind was clear
and my body calm.

Unfortunately, demons aren't as quick to dispel as their illusions.

Later that same night,
I woke up in claws.

It felt like my left ovary was being ripped out of my body.

The pain quite literally knocked me off my feet
—and kept me off them for a day.

Afterward, I was weak but determined.
For the demon usually attacked
when I took a step *away* from his control
and toward my own freedom.

Two days later, I met the man who had invited me to facilitate the retreat.
When we shook hands, Sarah flipped out, as did my stomach,
but I didn't understand why
she was having such an upsetting reaction to this kind man.

When I made it to dinner,
the man told me he had recruited men
in his community to guard me during the event.

My eyes widened in surprise, and my face flushed.
I had never had "guards" for an event before
and could not imagine *why* I might need them.

Despite my recent Redvelation
and my ample human protection,
the retreat had a rough start.

My self-doubt and stage fright shook me to pieces as usual.
And because I had made a point not to bring
my customary pile of copious notes, I had *no* idea what to do.

The participants became restless
and I sensed their disappointment.

My shoulders slumped
and my head dropped
in defeat.

But then I felt my Lady straighten my spine
and gently brush the hair away
from Sarah's downturned face,

letting us Know that
She Was Here
with us

no matter what happened
or did not happen.

And then I Realized if *She* was Here,
other Divine Souls were Here as well.

With a soft but firm voice, I asked the room
to make way for our Souls.

Then I began to support the reconnection
of each human with their distinct Divine Soul.

It was simple, natural, and oh-so-fucking beautiful.
It was the most Real thing I had ever had the honor to participate in.
And I Knew, without a doubt, that it was *Sarah's* Work.

Like the swell of a wave from the center of the ocean,
I felt the grace and the gift of Sarah's previous predicament and pain.

Only someone who has felt disconnected from her own Soul
can empathize and help others who might feel the same way.

For a brief moment, I was okay with Sarah's blemished past.
For a few hours, I felt okay exposing *both*
my humanity and my divinity publicly.
In other words, for a short while I was okay with just being myself.

Later that evening after the retreat,
when a few of us were kicking back
and jamming on musical instruments,

the man who had invited me and created the event
turned to me with tears in his eyes and said:

"I know how completely crazy this is going to sound,
but I feel like I need to say it anyway."

He took a big gulp of air.

"I invited you here because . . .
because I feel like I owe you something . . .
like, I owe *Sarah* something."

He exhaled and looked away from me
as he played a haunting, heart-ripping rhythm
on his handheld steel drum.

"I keep sensing that I was, like, some kind of guard for her and her mother.
And, I *remember* that I took her somewhere . . .
on a boat . . . through a cavern . . . to someone who was not to be trusted.
I did it out of greed . . . or something similar."

His hands never stopped beating softly on that drum.

He turned back toward me,
his eyes swirls of sorrow, shame, and regret,
and sputtered, "I'm sorry . . . I'm *so* sorry, Sarah."

My eyes matched his in wetness
as time collapsed between us.

We Saw each other as only souls can see.
We Felt each other as only souls can feel.

And then Sarah nodded.
His apology was accepted,
then and *now.*

We turned back toward the group,
ate some delicious Indian food,
and laughed the night away.

[pause]

Let me reiterate in case what happened wasn't clear:

a soul who *once*
took Sarah to her death place
because of her Soul's Work

created a safe-enough space for her
to bring her Soul's Work back to life,
now.

I don't know what else to call
this kind of thing
except Holy.

And I know in every fiber of my being
that this kind of Holiness is happening,
to each and every one of us,
whether we are conscious of it or not.

[deep breath]

There are forces inside and outside of us
that want us to think we're "crazy"
for having these kinds of experiences,

thereby succeeding in separating us from
the only Reality that can make us Whole.

We believe these forces
not only at the cost of our soul,
but also at the cost of our body
and this very planet.

We need to believe in
Something Bigger:
Ourselves.

Soul Pregnancy

Although the retreat provided
an enormous healing for my soul,

in the months following,
I grew sicker and sicker.

I saw holistic and allopathic doctors,
but no one could determine the cause
or could help me feel better.

I was chronically nauseated, fatigued, and dizzy.
I woke up around 3:00 a.m. almost every night
feeling so ill that I was unable to go back to sleep.

I couldn't sleep or eat,
exercise or work,
much less socialize.

I got to such a weak point that I knew,
in that deep-down belly kind of way,
that if this continued,
I wouldn't.

One night, as I lay awake begging for some relief,
I received an image that I was pregnant

not with a child,
but with this book.

Then I heard a whisper:
"I need to tell my story."

I recognized the voice.
It was Sarah's.

This was an unwanted
and unplanned pregnancy,
for sure.

And I reacted as such.

I had just spent three years cooped up in the Red tent
birthin' my second book, and I was biting at the bit
to stop focusing on myself
and start doing more spiritual activism and service work.

I had also included Sarah in *Red Hot and Holy*
and was letting her do her Work (secretly) during my public events.
So why did I have to write an entire fucking book about her?

Before she came into my life, I was a happy woman who had her shit together.
Working with Sarah was like living with a dark cloud hanging over me.
She was so goddamn depressing, dramatic, and needy,
and she was messing with my career and making me sick!

Why couldn't she behave like a normal soul fragment,
or *whatever* she was,
get over herself and her crappy life already,
and let me get on with *my* life?

As I stomped my feet in this puddle of petulancy,
my Lady decided to drop a gargantuan truth bomb
that exploded my sense of self and Sarah.

Bombs Away

Sarah is much more than a soul fragment.
Sarah constitutes the majority of your human soul,

and you cannot effectively contribute to this planet,
nor can your body continue living,
without her.

You are the part of Sarah's soul
that moved forward and experienced other lifetimes,
while she stayed left behind.

You are Sarah's only piece in present time,
and you are the only one who can bring her home.

One way is through remembering
and writing her story,
which is also your story.

You will write your soul back into your body,
and you will save both *of your lives*
in the process.

My Lady finished
by making the hand gesture
of a bomb going off:

BOOM!

Reverberations

What was even more shocking than *what* my Lady boomed
was that the truth She spoke resounded through my body
like it had always been there.

Like my body had been patiently holding
my soul's truth for me
until my conscious mind could catch up
and my ego could handle it.

Holy shit monkeys, I thought.
I am not who I think I am.

I am not some flexible, independent creature
who is creating her own reality (woot woot!).

My current existence is the rigid result
of a past reality.
I'm the runoff of a runaway soul.

My meeting with Marion Woodman
replayed itself from a new angle.

Losing my soul was not just a psychological condition,
a slogan for a misdirected career, or even a mystical crisis.
It was also a metaphysical matter.

Most of me was not *here.*
Most of me was tied up in the past.

And, although I had been going back
and untying Sarah knot by knot,

I still didn't feel intimately connected with life,
with other humans, or with my body.

Sarah and I were both still separate and suffering.

But remembering and writing down
my soul's *entire* story
would stimulate a whole other kind of suffering.

Because it required that I face and feel
everything I have avoided facing and feeling.

As the saying goes: we can run, but we can't hide.
Eventually the past will catch up with us . . .
and, uh, impregnate us.

Every mother knows birth is painful.
But it's the only way to bring forth new life.

It was time to birth Sarah back to Life.

And, in so doing,
I would come back to Life.

The Catalyst

To catalyze this process,
my partner of three years went to India
and fell for another woman.

And then he fell for another woman
after he returned to the States.

It was as if the ground fell
from under my feet
and took my heart with it.

Now my partner did not physically act on his feelings,
but nonetheless I was besieged by *my* wounded feelings of
rejection, abandonment, betrayal, and feeling unlovable
just to name a few.

While these are common feelings to have when your
partner strays physically, emotionally, or energetically,
the force of them was a clue that what I was reacting to
was not primarily based in present time.

Years before, right after my encounter with Marion Woodman,
my boyfriend at the time *also* fell for another woman.

Back then, I did everything I could
to quash my extreme feelings
because they did not seem very "spiritual."

They made me feel flawed and vulnerable,
unattractive and wrong.

Feeling my feelings felt *way* too risky.
In so doing, I would surely lose the man and the life
I was desperately trying to hold onto.

Also, I did not understand the difference
between emoting and feeling.

Emoting skims our surface.
Feeling comes from our core.

Emoting might temporarily release something in us,
but feeling permanently transmutes us.

It's a bit like a champagne bottle popping
versus a volcano erupting.

One sprays all over the place and needs to be wiped up.
The other explodes due to natural pressure and creates new land.

Although emoting can make a mess,
feeling threatens our life.

Point is: my unwillingness to feel is a pattern.

For most of my adult life, I kept myself busy:
focusing on my partner and the needs of the people I was aiming to serve;
writing books, giving retreats, and following my vocation;
fixing—er, "improving"—myself via health regimens,
relationship books, and antiaging lotions;
analyzing myself psychologically and awakening myself spiritually.

In other words: I do everything I can, including
spiritual, psychological, and service work,
in order *not* to face and feel
my soul's wounds.

But there's been a black hole at the bottom
of all my clever coping mechanisms.

A black hole that my boyfriend
unknowingly pushed me toward,
even though in reality
I'd been getting sucked into it
for a while.

Through the lens of my soul,
the situation with my boyfriend
offered me another chance
to face and feel my soul's wounds.

Through the lens of my ego
nothing appeared more threatening.

Our egos have built
multilayered defenses
around our wounds.

Our defenses are incredibly helpful
and absolutely necessary.

They allow us to grow strong enough
to eventually handle our big feelings.
They help us float without drowning.

But

they also prevent us from fully Living and fully Loving.
To Live and to Love means we have to be willing to
sink to the bottom and *feel*.

When we are ready.

Apparently, I was ready.
I had reached a point where I was
safe and strong enough
to face and feel my soul's wounds.

I had also reached a point
where the pain of avoiding my wounds
had grown close in proportion
to the pain of actually feeling them.

Though I could leave my boyfriend,
which my ego felt justified to do,
I knew now that he wasn't
the *source* of my pain.

My wounds had been with me *long* before
my boyfriend had entered my life
and would still be there if he exited my life.

Needless to say, there was nowhere else to go
but into the black hole of my soul.

Feelings

One evening, after another distressing conversation
with my boyfriend, I felt the familiar pain start to rise.

But instead of defending myself against it,
I decided to allow myself to feel it.

With concentrated effort,
I let down my defenses
and waited for impact.

The pain started to come in waves,
pushing me down,
filling my lungs,
and breaking across my body.

Right when I thought things were calming,
another wave would crash over me,
making it hard to breathe or reach the surface.

Although I had felt pain before,
a lot of it actually,
this pain felt different,
and more than what I previously knew as pain.

My hands began to make
sweeping gestures
down my heaving chest.

I moaned and moved,
swore and struggled

to stay with the pain as best I could
while my boyfriend watched me,
holding his hands over his heart.

Although part of me felt embarrassed,
a wiser part of me knew that
there was something significant
and even *sacred* going on here,
and I needed a witness.

Through feeling my feelings,
I was beginning to Incarnate.
I was starting to become human.

In Body

While I continued to stay in and work on my relationship,
this process eventually required a bigger container.

Call it Lady Luck, a gobsmacking blessing,
or "I must have done something in a past life"
(sorry, it had to be said at some point),

but my loving and generous aunt and uncle gifted me
with a four-month stay at their beautiful, vacated condo
outside Charleston, South Carolina.

I needed this place like a fetus needs an umbilical cord.

It was here that I started to write Sarah's story
over a tidal marsh
bursting with dolphins, frogs, wood storks,
and the pungent smell of pluff mud.

Every night after I finished writing,
I would drive to the nearby beach on Sullivan's Island
where I would float in the endless motion of Her Oceanic Body,
then crawl onto Her soft sands and *feel my body.*

I discovered for myself
what many wise ones know:
My body is my soul's story.

My facial asymmetry and curved shoulders;
twisted left side and extra-tight hamstrings;
difficulty keeping on weight; narrow, resistant feet;
weak muscles; and a mitral-valve prolapsed heart
are some of the physical reflections of my
soul's experiences and my disembodiment.

For the body and soul belong together.

When they are separate they become susceptible
to all kinds of structural abnormalities, ailments, and attacks.

And no supplement, bodywork, yoga, healthy diet and lifestyle,
allopathic medicine, or alternative healing modality
can help my body unless I'm *also* working with my soul.

Likewise, no amount of spiritual, psychological, energetic, or soul work
can help me unless I'm *also* working with my body,
receiving its unrivaled wisdom and following its trustworthy guidance.

Our body, like our soul, has Organic Intelligence.

Our body stores our memories and feelings,
but it also knows unerringly how to release them.

There are noises it can make:
whispers and roars, whistles and chants,
sobs and laughter, sighs and moans,
snorts and gasps, slaps and claps.

There are movements it can make:
fast and slow, chaotic and rhythmic,
animalistic and ethereal.

To help us release our feelings
and express our soul
through our body,
there is Nature.

Oh, *Mama.*

Her Body *always* surrounds us
as a park or a backyard,
mountains, desert, woods, beaches.

Her vibrant shoots of green even rebelliously
break through concrete,
flashing us along highways and strip malls.

A soul suggestion:
put some bare skin on Her,
at least once a day.

Feel Her unremitting support,
Her Wide-Open Welcome of Your All.

Let Her teach you how to be Wild again
and mirror back your primal perfection.

After I felt and released what was needed each night,
I began to move in ways I never had before.

The movements I made on that beach
were native and natural,
uniquely my own,
and they changed like the weather.

Some nights, I grabbed at and gobbled up
the salty fresh air around me
like it was a vitamin I was severely deficient in.

Other times, I forcefully pushed away
anything unnatural that had been "fed" to me,
lifetime after lifetime.

Occasionally I stomped and growled,
shoving my feet deep into the sand,
marking my physical territory,
wordlessly declaring my right to be here.

Often, I would bring my iPod,
hit "shuffle" (allowing the Divine to be my DJ),
and dance my ass off with the elements.

Sometimes when I made it to that beach,
I was too tired to move much at all
and I poured myself onto the ground.

Lying there,
my human body
surrendered to
and supported by
Her earthly Body,

I Remembered
how it *first* felt
to Be Here,

with Her
and
in Her.

In the safety of my Mother's Womb,
I was nourished, revitalized,
and lovingly reintroduced to physicality.

This was how I wrote Sarah's story.
And this was how I became ready to Return.

It's Time

One day, as I shut down my computer I heard:

It's Time to Return.

I had no idea what my Lady was talking about,
but my body sure did because I almost threw up.

Attempting to calm my queasy belly,
I asked my Lady to be a bit less cryptic.

And that's when it felt like a stretched-out,
two-thousand-year-old rubber band
was snapping me

back

into a place I never,
ever,
wanted to return to.

There's a theory that intentionally returning
to the past will change our present.

The belief is that we can re-experience, re-enact, or reimagine
difficult or traumatic past events in a more conscious and empowering way,
thereby creating a happier and healthier present life.

Although I *had* been practicing feeling my wounds
and releasing my feelings in helpful ways,
I had not returned to their Source.

And although I had been writing as Sarah,
I had also been keeping my distance, as Sera.
My Lady's message meant no more distance.

So, I reacted like any normal person would
when told it was time
to merge with a suffering soul fragment
and return to the Source of their greatest pain.

The Explosion

"This is fucking bullshit!" I shout
  at my Lady and the Universe at large.

"Why do I have to return to *her* life?!
Why do you keep pushing me into *Sarah's* pain?!"

I'm only pushing you into yourself, my Lady answers.

I throw my hands up in the air,
"This whole thing is crazy-making!"

It is soul-making.

"Oh really?" I shoot back, "Cause this feels like needless suffering."

I know it can feel that way sometimes.

"No you don't! You really, *really* don't!" I spit.

My rage rips through time,
leveling the self-imposed walls
between Sarah and Sera,

closing the distance between us
and opening two millennia worth
of pent-up sentiments.

"And you certainly don't know
what it was like
to be there
when It All went down!!!" I yell.

You are angry, Sarah.

"Uh, 'angry' doesn't quite cover it, Lady!

Not only did I experience
the bitter and brutal ending
of my family,

but I have since witnessed the erasure of my Lineage
and the extermination of those devoted to It!

So now historians and archaeologists can find little
to no physical evidence of my parents' marriage or my Lineage,

and scholars can only posit tentative theories based on partial,
eroded, unorthodox, and thereby *unacceptable* texts.

When a popular novel, oral legend, or piece of papyrus shakes things up,
most regard it as fictional, unreliable, fake, or sensationalist.

This book I'm writing will most likely be as unwelcome and harshly judged,
as I was when I slid out between my mother's legs!

Those who take my parents' marriage seriously are seen as
misguided at best, delusional at least, and demonic at worst
—not to mention kooky conspiracy theorists or flakes.

Then, there's the cosmic influence and imposters
and New Age portrayals of my parents,
which have become almost worse than the Church!
There are *thousands* of supposed 'jesuses' and 'magdalenes'
beaming down or strutting around.

And, don't even get me started on the bloodline bullshit!

My family has been inflated into archetypes, ascended masters, and saviors
with heady books, cheesy channelings, and unreachable proportions.

And they've been deflated into psychotherapeutic complexes,
myths, symbols, and creative exercises
—imprisoned in the psyche or relegated to the imaginal.

The Truth of Us
now registers as the *false* in us
or the not quite real.

So much so
that even
I doubt
if we were Real.

So much so
that I doubt
if I am Real."

I choke on an ocean of fire
as I feel just how furious
I am at humanity

for treating me like I don't exist!

For buying the lies
and perpetuating my prison!

For leaving me
underground
by myself!

My Lady cuts in: *What do you want to say to the world, Sarah?*

"I EXIST!!!"
I roar and slap my chest.

"I!
[*slap*]

FUCKING!
[*slap*]

EXIST!!!"
[*slap*]

My head drops,
my stinging hands leave my chest
and find my thighs, my nails dig deep.

"Even though I fucked it up, I still deserve my own life!
Even though I'm ashamed of what I did, I was still there!
I was with them! I was their daughter!
Goddamnit! I haven't even been allowed my own suffering!"

A spark ignites within my first fetus body
and I allow it to grow and grow
into a *raging* fire

that blazes through every body I've ever had,
collecting momentum and gaining power
until it hits my present-day body.

I open my
bodysoulmouth
and I

EXPLODE!!!

The sound shocks me.
It's unlike anything I have ever heard.
It blasts through my body and this reality.
It shakes my muscles and the walls.
It burns so hot that I smell smoke and taste ash.

When the explosion finishes,
I feel like I must be, too.

But my Lady gently coaxes,
What else angers you?

Another surge fills my body.
"Every time I walk into a church,
it reminds me that we lost and *they* won!
All I want to do is smash the crucifix!"

Why don't you imagine doing so, my Lady suggests.

I grab a large wooden spoon from the kitchen and run to the bedroom
where I fervently beat the pillows and mattress with everything I've got left,
all the while imagining that I'm smashing a crucifix to smithereens.

When I'm thoroughly wiped out,
I sink to the floor in a swirl of feathers.
Staring at my reddened, sore hands,
I start to sob.

As my wise Lady knew,
fully expressed rage
opens a doorway to grief.

I grieve for Sarah and as Sarah.
I weep for everything and everyone that was lost.
I cry like I have needed to for two thousand years.

After a good, long, wet while,
I mumble through a mound of soggy tissues:

"Because Christianity is a positive source for many,
    it's felt more compassionate, evolved, and just plain easier
    to ignore my feelings and memories and keep my mouth shut."

[blowing my nose]

"But I have done so *at the cost of my own soul.*"

My Lady softly offers: *Your soul's truth*
might be different than others' truth,
but it still has the right to be shared.
So tell us more of your truth . . .

Embers from my heart fly out of my mouth.

"The Church has us focusing up, at Him,
    instead of also down, at *Her*
    and inward, at *Ourselves.*

Most people can acknowledge
    that the Feminine has been excluded,
    but if I'm also missing at that cross,
    then *every Soul is missing*!

The Church's crucifix is *one piece* of Our Whole Truth!
It's a misrepresentation of the Nature of this Universe!

How can we Liberate and Love
ourselves, each other, and this planet
if we have no Real examples of

> The Divine Masculine
> *in Love*
> with
> the Divine Feminine
> *holding*
> their Divine Child?

Metaphors, myths, symbols, deities, and archetypes
are potent, helpful, and indispensable,
but *nothing* beats genuine human experience!

And *that's* what my parents exemplified
more than anything else: human beings in Love!"

My Lady murmurs:

So Sarah,
go be a human
in Love
with them.

Sacred Wound

Immediately an inner guard forms a blockade
around what feels like the basement of my being

and the place I need to go in order to
"be a human in Love."

I suddenly feel like a trespasser in my own home.
My consciousness is unwanted and setting off alarms.

"What's down there?" I breathlessly ask my Lady.

Your Sacred Wound, Sarah.

This is different than the Wound of Incarnation,
which is the wound every soul receives
when they first feel the intensity
of being incarnate on earth.

The Sacred Wound is more intimate and personal
and usually inflicted by those closest to you.
It is the Wound of your wounds.

"Oh, is that all?" I half-jokingly respond
and then mutter, "No wonder I detest basements."

To be human is to be wounded, Sera.
It is a difficult, but important, part of Life.

While there are many ways around your wounds,
the Way of Love is through them.

After years of working with Sarah,
I had become more familiar with my wounds,
but becoming conscious of my Sacred Wound
—the Wound that initiated *all* my wounds—
feels almost unendurable, and it appears impenetrable.

Not only is my inner guard surrounding the wound
but I sense a prowler too:
the demon.

Surprised, I ask my Divine Soul:
"Why is the demon hanging around my Sacred Wound?
Is it because he relishes my pain?"

*There are different kinds of pain
one experiences in life.*

*Interfering forces like the demon
create synthetic darkness,
inflict unnatural and undue pain,
and cause unnecessary destruction.*

*This kind of interference, as well as
abuse, cruelty, and physical pain
are* not *the kinds of pain
one needs to re-experience.*

*The pain one is encouraged to feel,
when they are ready,
is a* natural *pain
that comes from
the organic experience of being human.*

If resisted, this natural pain becomes stuck.

*It blocks the flow of Life and Love,
preventing the soul from healing, evolving,
and expressing what it originally came here to express.*

*The demon pokes and prods your wounds,
but he does* not *want you to face
and fully feel your soul's wounds.*

Because he knows that will be the beginning of his end.

He knows that re-entering
your Sacred Wound
is how you re-enter yourself.

Now *that* revs my engines.
My demon is my greatest adversary.

He has been tailing me and targeting me for two millennia,
doing every clever thing he can,
including coming through the shadows of those closest to me
in order to keep me separate from my Red Soul.

Maybe *this* is how I finally release his grip.

I reapproach my inner guards.
"Let me enter," I demand.
My guards cross their arms.

I try a new approach, "OK, I won't enter
my Sacred Wound *yet*,
but at least let me go down the stairs."

The guards shift and I move past them,
into the depths of my depths
until I encounter my Sacred Wound,
pulsing with unfiltered pain.

Like my Wound of Incarnation,
my Sacred Wound happened
during the crucifixion,
specifically
when I felt abandoned by my parents.

Although I do not enter my Sacred Wound,
the feeling of it is so dire,
so disheartening, so devoid of *any* light
that I have to pull myself back
in order not to sink into hopeless oblivion.

It's not easy to find words for this feeling,
but here is my best attempt:

My Sacred Wound is feeling unloved *by Love Itself.*

At some point, every child
experiences feeling unloved
by those closest to them.
I was no different.

But my soul took this common experience particularly hard
because those who wounded me by "not loving me"
were Jesus and Magdalene

whom my soul recognized and experienced
as the Divine Masculine and Divine Feminine
embodiments of True Love on Earth.

So if I wasn't loved by *Them*,
then how could I be loved
by anyone or anything?

I felt so far beyond unlovable,
I was off the map.

The feeling was insufferable,
so I protected myself.

I sealed my heart shut
and have avoided True Love
ever since.

And I chose false love,
the kind my demon offered me.

Yes, false love has hurt me,
but True Love has *destroyed* me.

There is something else I become aware of:
an unconscious belief about myself
that was formed in reaction
to my Sacred Wound.

As a fetus, I felt there had to be a reason *why*
I was unloved by Love Itself.

And the reason I came up with was
that it must be because
I am an *evil* soul.

This previously unconscious belief about myself helps explain
why I first rejected and sold my Soul in the womb
and why it was so easy for that man to convince me
that Red was evil and poisoning True Love
when I was in that underground cell.

It also hasn't helped that evil
is often depicted as Red.

In fact, a former close friend of mine told me
just before *Red Hot and Holy* was to be published
that she psychically sensed that my Red Lady
was malevolent.

It felt like my universe imploded.
I could barely function
and almost pulled the book.

Now I know why.

My friend shot a bullet directly into my Sacred Wound
right when I was about to reveal my Red Soul to the world.

This is another example of a *trans-incarnational* unconscious
that stays with us lifetime after lifetime,
often attracting or recreating similar situations in each life
thereby providing opportunities to discover and heal the original wounds.

With that in mind, it's important to share
a bit more about the nature of core wounds.

Psychologists know that core wounds can happen at any time,
but tend to occur when we are between zero to two years old,
which means we can be wounded while in the womb.

We become wounded from many different things, such as
not being picked up *one* time when we are crying in our crib, ongoing neglect,
abuse, the absence of a parent, preferential treatment of a sibling during a fight,
or overhearing a family member say something unkind about us, and so on.

Because most of us are wounded at such a young age,
it's not biologically safe for us to blame our caregivers (yet)
because they are our only means of survival and appear like gods to us
(Whom am I to blame? Jesus and Magdalene?).

So we blame ourselves instead.

We come up with a reason for why this has happened to us,
which usually results in the belief that
it happened because something is (very) *wrong* with us.

We create these false beliefs about ourselves
often when we are *preverbal*.

However, as adults it's important to become conscious of,
and try to verbalize, the beliefs that formed in reaction to the wound
because they influence our decisions, generate our behaviors,
and stimulate our strategies.

Most commonly, we try to prove that we are the *opposite*
of our wound-based beliefs,
which often propels us to do what we do in life (or our lives).

So for example, if we unconsciously believe we are worthless,
we will try to prove that we *are* valuable and strive to be
the *best* financier, mother, spiritual teacher, surgeon, or coach.

In reaction to my Sacred Wound,
I have done my best to prove that I am not "evil"
by trying to be as "spiritual" as possible,
and my humanity has suffered enormously as a result.

I've also worked myself to the bone
in order to be loved again by Love Itself.

[deep breath]

When we are ready to become aware of
our core wounds and resulting false beliefs
and we recognize how we've been living our life
(or lives) in reaction to them,
we need to be extra-gentle with ourselves,
because it's *a lot* to take in.

At this point in my process, I call "mercy,"
and temporarily shut the door on the soul realm.

I take long walks on the beach and play with dogs,
eat some good ol' Southern comfort food,
and watch comedy shows . . . for a few weeks.

Soul work demands soul play,
soul food, and goofy humor.

If all my soul work is getting too much for you,
I suggest you close this book,
do something fun and nourishing,
and join me again, later.

Shadows

I hope you took a healthy break
because things are only intensifying
from here on out.

When I felt ready to enter the soul realm again,
I tiptoed down into the basement of my being.

Lurking around my wounds
were my trans-incarnational shadows
—disowned parts of me that developed
in reaction to my first life and that want to:

judge, critique, and condemn others so they feel
as evil, unlovable, and unwanted as I have felt;
abuse my power after feeling so powerless: *"Kneel bastards!"*;
and tear down other people's missions that threaten my own unlived one.

And then there is my *cosmic* shadow.

[low whistle]

This is the part of my shadow
that exists in the cosmic dimension,
but influences this earthly dimension.

My cosmic shadow-queen wants to receive
everything that she feels Sarah *deserves*:
prestige, praise, fame, worship.

She believes that she is better than you and humanity and All of This.
She even thinks she is better than the Creator and Creatrix of this Universe.

[gulp]

I have hurt myself and many beings via my shadows,
which stem from my soul's core wounds,
and this has been a huge motivation for me to face my past
and start the process of healing it.

My shadow work is ongoing.
However, I am a Being
of *both* light and dark.

Glorifying or hiding
either
ain't my Soul's style.

Being Real *is*.

Too Much

Admittedly at this point in my process,
it all just feels like *too much*.

I mean if this is what we humans are up against
—fetal trauma, core wounds, false beliefs, past lives,
and multidimensional shadows (that are all unconscious!)—

plus

injustice, wars, environmental devastation, disease,
poverty, synthetic spirituality, oppositional forces,
and not to mention freakin' *demons*—

how does any of us stand a chance?

I've been afforded the time, energy, and means
and I'm *still* struggling,
so how do others who are dealing with *much* harder
and even horrific life situations embody their soul?

Becoming human feels like an impossible feat,
and *being* human, with all its struggles, pain, and suffering,
doesn't seem like a very fair or worthwhile gig.

You Chose This, my Lady interrupts.

"You did NOT just say that!" I bellow back with outrage.

"You're gonna tell that crack baby or rape victim
or Native American forced on a reservation or African slave or Holocaust survivor
or girl growing up in the slums or grieving mother who just lost her child
or bullied transgender teenager or bipolar homeless person or cancer patient
or the millions of humans who can barely find food
and are just trying to—oh I don't know—*survive*
that they *chose* this?!

That's the kind of unhelpful and *damaging* parlance
used by sanctimonious, privileged spiritual people!"

I'm not talking about other souls or their paths.
I'm talking about you and your path.

I sweep through my life as Sarah
and every life since,
then vigorously shake my head.

"Well, if this is what I 'chose,'
then fucking take my ability
to choose *away*!"

The You Who Chose This was Me,
your Divine Soul.

"So, a Divine Soul, who had
never been incarnate before
chose my lives.
That makes me feel better," I snort.

"Piece of advice from your human:
don't choose a life
until you've actually experienced one!"

My Lady gracefully moves on.
You cannot be told why you chose This.
You can only be encouraged to Remember.

And you cannot Remember
with your mind.

You can only Remember
through your Heart.

So let's Remember Together.

The Choice

My Lady places Her hand on my heart.

My spinning mind slows down
as my heart heats up.

Its ever-present warmth
and always-available wisdom

start to grow
and fill me,

Reminding me of the different dimensions of choice.

There are the choices I make as a human soul,
like how I chose to reject my Soul and my mission
in my first lifetime—and in every lifetime since.

But beyond that dimension,
and beyond a few more after that,

I begin to Remember and feel a *much* Bigger Choice
than all my other choices combined:

The Choice I have made as a Divine Soul to Become Human.

Everything inside me recognizes this Choice.

My cells carry It,
my blood circulates It,
my spine aligns to It.

Becoming human is one of the main reasons
I chose to enter this Universe in the first place.

Living as an infinite, eternal Divine Being
with finite, temporary flesh
and feeling and experiencing everything this entails
is an unparalleled, rare, and *precious* opportunity.

[pause]

None of this was coming from my mind
or some "higher state of consciousness"
or spiritual sentimentality.

These are words I'm now giving to
a fresh and fearless *Memory*
I have always held in my heart
and felt in my body.

While my Choice to become human feels true,
my human mind can't help but wonder
if my Being is just an experience junkie?

There *has* to be more to it.

Because the desire to experience things like:

birth and death, friendship and betrayal, separation and fear,
trauma and wounds, roses and thorns, earlobes and armpits,
fighting and dancing, artichokes and whale songs, dogs and dogs,
sunsets and thunderstorms, sex and hugs, burping and farting, bad haircuts,
swimming in the ocean and hiking in the mountains, singing in the shower,
mud between the toes and snowflakes on the tongue, holding hands, bee stings,
laughing so hard you pee your pants and crying so hard you see stars,
cherry pie and chipmunks, forgetting and then remembering,
shattering into pieces and then becoming whole again,

when one hasn't before is one thing.

But why did I choose
to experience pain and suffering
lifetime after lifetime?

My heart goes off like a multiverse of fireworks.

Oh . . .

I Chose to feel pain
and experience suffering,
lifetime after lifetime

to expand and evolve my capacity *to Love.*

Loving in the Divine realms is easy.
Loving as a Divine Being is effortless.

Loving in the earthly realm is *not* easy.
Loving as a human being takes effort.
And practice. Lots and lots of practice.

Becŏming human
is the
Ultimate Teaching,
Training,
and Test of Love.

Can I Love even when
what I'm experiencing feels like
the *opposite* of It?

Can I Love even when I am suffering
or witnessing others suffering?

Can I Love when I can't feel or find Love, *anywhere?*

Choosing to be at the crucifixion
suddenly makes "Soul Sense."

I've held a false belief that love
will protect me from pain and suffering,
but True Love *includes* pain and suffering.

Through this Whole-Hearted Perspective and Feeling,
I *needed* the Wound of Incarnation I received by life
and the Sacred Wound I received by my parents
in order to learn how to Truly Love as a human on earth.

In other words, during the crucifixion
I experienced what I wanted to experience as a Divine Soul
and I received what I needed to receive as a human soul.

Not to mention I witnessed Love in Action.

The Creator and Creatrix Incarnated
to show us *how*
to Love

in Their Body
and in our body.

They taught through example
how to be True Love in the flesh.

They demonstrated
that it's *not* easy,
but it *is* possible.

Through my Heart, I now Understand
that my parents *had* to focus
solely on each other at the crucifixion.

For not only could I not learn to Love
without my wounds,
but neither could they.

This Truth, Their Truth, *Love's* Truth,
reframed my abandonment at the cross
and forgiveness found me and freed them.

Remembering and feeling my Choice
to become human and experience all facets of life,
including the crucifixion,
sanctified my soul's foundation.

I stopped playing the violins for myself and asking, "Why me?"
I didn't blindly grab the shortest straw in the bunch.
I Chose my straw with eyes wide open.

[pause]

I am not declaring that this is true *for you*
or that it explains why you or others have suffered.

There is far more complexity and mystery
behind human suffering
than I am capable of knowing or sharing in this book.

Please do not let what I organically Remembered for myself
become another spiritual belief to use against yourself or others:
"Oh, I/they *chose* to be raped or to get cancer."

If there is more for you to know about your suffering
it will be revealed in its own time,
from inside you.

Although Remembering my Soul's Choice
doesn't make much sense to my mind,

end my pain, heal my wounds,
take away my trauma, or make Life easier,

it *does* remind me that I can handle
and *trust* whatever happens.

Love is behind It All,
even if It appears
so very far away.

I take a deep breath from
every set of lungs I've ever had
and then exhale.

I feel ready to rejoin Life
and my human and holy Family.

I am ready to Return
for Love.

The Return

A few nights later, I go to the beach
and plop down in the sand with my iPod.

I don't exactly know *how* to "Return,"
but I press "play" on my iPod
and David Tolk's exquisite piece
"In Reverence" begins.

As I listen to the music
a motion starts in my pelvis:
a gentle rocking

back and forth,
forth and back.

There and here,
here and there.

My body falls backward onto the sand
and I feel the earth's solid support.

I turn over on all fours
and start crawling

back

through my lives,
starting with this one.

I move through the Red tent and my meeting with Marion Woodman,
through my relationships, my career, my travels, my studies,
my childhood in Atlanta.

I continue to move backward,
through a hellish concentration camp and heavenly convents,
a cramped slave ship and sweltering cotton fields,
isolated caves and teeming temples.

I crawl over battlefields and piles of my banned books.
Through courtrooms, castles, and the Inquisition,
acknowledging when my own hands are stained red.

I make my way toward bonfires where I have burned
and through jails where I have been tortured,
over cliffs where I have leapt,
and around trees where I have hung.

I glide through several lives
where I've felt content and at ease.

Like the North American plains where I have run freely, feathers flying;
the Himalayas where I have found peace, mind calming;
and the jungles of India where I have loved brazenly, body smiling.

As I crawl through the timeline of my lives,
I catch the eyes of my previous incarnations.

Each of them,
no matter what painful or pleasurable state they are in,
nod knowingly at me, encouraging me
to keep going.

Finally, I feel where it all began.
My body trembles
and my breath becomes shallow.

I pause, gather all the positive resources
I have received from my past incarnations
and then re-enter my first life.

At first, it's just an inky haze.

Then the smell of torn flesh meets my nose
mixed with the sounds of a riotous crowd
and the chaotic forces of violence.

I am back at the Crucifixion.

I resolutely raise up
from my hands and knees
onto shaking legs.

The energy heightens
as the haze clears around
the Center of It All:

My parents.

Who are staring straight at me.
Like they have been *waiting* for me.

Sarah, you've Returned!

In this timeless moment, it's blatantly evident
that my parents didn't abandon me at this cross;
I abandoned them.

I burst into tears, and my legs start moving.
I'm coming, Papa! I'm coming, Mama!

I shove my way through the crowd
and break free from the guards,
just like my mama has done,

until there is nothing
and no one else
between us.

First I go to my father,
for he doesn't have much time left.

I tenderly bring my forehead to his mangled feet.
"I'm so sorry, Papa; I'm *so* sorry for leaving you."

We have a private exchange
that communicates the indescribable Love
between a father and daughter.

When we are done,
I crouch down
next to my mama.

I brush her matted hair away from her streaked face,
wrap my arms around her wailing body,
and offer my wordless apology.

One of her strong arms pries loose
from the base of the cross,
and hugs me to her,
tight.

It's the Three of Us.
Three humans hangin' in there together
and Loving the hell out of each other.

I feel a flutter in my mama's womb
from my frightened fetus soul.

I beckon this fragment
back into my body,
but she refuses to budge.

She communicates that I need
to come inside *her* body.

So, I do.

Immediately, everything goes black.

My suffering, grief, and terror are still here.
But I know I can handle them now.

For I am both that innocent fetus, Sarah,
and the wise adult, Sera,

who trusts her body and her Soul
and the Life She has Chosen for Herself.

I was made for This.

I enter my Wounds I received at the cross:
the Wound of Incarnation and my Sacred Wound.

Instantly, Pain batters my present-day body,
which curls into the fetal position on the beach.

It comes in forceful blows,
roughly knocking me about.

I clutch and claw at the sand,
raggedly breathe in and out,
and start to moan.

There is nowhere to hide from this Pain,
and there is no way to prevent it.

It is always here.

It affects everything and everyone.

It is Life on Earth.

I start shaking in shock
as my nervous system levels
any remaining spiritual loftiness
until there is nothing left to hold onto.

Nothing.

My heart stops and my breath halts.

This is It.
My Sacred Wound.

This is the feeling that I have avoided feeling for two thousand years.

It is harder to feel than I ever could have imagined
and totally different than what I ever could have thought.

It is existing *without* Love.

[pause]
[pause]
[pause]

Out of the darkness,
an alluring being approaches me,
exuding care and comfort,
love and light.

He clucks sympathetically
and tells me
that Sarah isn't real.

History proves
that Jesus and Magdalene
were *not* in love
and never had a child.

So, he gently asks,
why experience
unnecessary suffering?

All I have to do is say the word,
and he will take this painful
and dangerous *delusion*
away.

Then, he assures me, I will feel better,
my life will get back on track,
and I can *really* help this planet.

Abruptly,
my Natural Instincts
take over.

My left arm shoots out,
hand flexed back,
fingers spread wide:

"STOP!!!" I ferociously growl,
spit shooting out of my mouth.

"This is *MY* PAIN!
This is *MY* SOUL!
This is *MY* LIFE!

You will not take ANY of this from me!
I have made MY CHOICE!"

My right arm raises above my head,
hand curling into a fist,

"I
AM
STAYING
HERE!!!"

My right arm
drops,
and my fist
slams
the ground.

The demon bows and backs away
and I gasp with relief.

I Feel It All and It is *Magnificent.*

I'm being bitten by dozens of hungry mosquitos on the beach.
Snot, sweat, and sand have formed a gooey paste in my hair.
I'm crying and laughing, swatting and swearing at the same time.

My heart feels expansive and full,
here *and there.*

It beats loud and proud
within my mother's womb at the cross,
matching her own heartbeat,
and learning from it.

Then my father exhales his last breath,
and *that's* when the first Miracle happens,
not three days later.

In the darkest,
most painful
moment of their lives,

his heart and her heart
don't shut

but

*BLAST
OPEN!*

So,

All of Existence

FEELS

the Undeniable Reality

and

Unbeatable Power

of

TRUE LOVE.

BOOM!!!

No matter what has happened in the mixed-up
and messy two millennia that have followed,
or what religion or nonreligion we participate in,

this Epic Demonstration
and
Eternal Declaration

beats and burns

inside each and every one of us.

We have *all* received the wounds of Jesus,
the wounds of his wife,
and the wounds of their daughter.

They are Humanity's Wounds.
They are the Wounds of Life.

And we have all received
the Reason and Remedy for them:

True Love.

It is why and how
our Souls came into this Universe
and incarnated onto this planet.

And,
True Love
is

What

Holds
Us
All
Together.

[deep breath]

Back at the beach,
my body continues to release.

My tailbone untucks
and my chest stretches open
to Receive Life.

Red starts to flow
from between my thighs
and into the earth.

I stand up,
take off my clothes,
and widen my legs.

With my right hand,
I reach down
and gather my blood.

I place my Red hand on my forehead:

In the name of my Father,

I move my Red hand down to my belly,

my Mother,

I rub my Red hand around my red heart,

and All of Us.

I dip my pointer and middle fingers
between my legs
and paint Red streaks under my eyes.

My Soul's Warrior marks.

I walk to the ocean
and let my beloved body
be washed by gentle waves.

When the cleansing is done,
I spontaneously break into what feel like
primal cheerleading moves,
finishing with a triumphant pose:

"TOUCH DOWN!"

BREAK TIME

The Exorcism

On Mother's Day, a few months *before* my fetus soul retrieval,
I sat next to a radiant woman at a yoga retreat
who shared with me that she had recently undergone
an exceptional kind of surgery for endometriosis.

Endometriosis is a chronic, painful disease
in which the endometrium tissue grows outside the uterus
where it can adhere to the pelvic wall
and negatively affect and even penetrate several organs.

Due to my occasional, but debilitating, episodes during my periods
(always after a nightmare about a nefarious being attacking me)
I suspected I suffered from endometriosis,
but it could only be confirmed through surgery.

The woman told me that this highly successful
surgical technique was called excision,
and it was originally conceived by a Dr. *Redwine.*

He created the technique because his wife
suffered from endometriosis
and traditional surgeries weren't helping.
It was created out of Love.

On that Mother's Day, I knew I was given a directive.

However, it wasn't till months *after*
my soul retrieval at the crucifixion
that I scheduled the surgery.

Being a holistic gal who tends to eschew allopathic medicine,
choosing to have elective surgery was unnerving, to say the least.

But every time I doubted myself
the signs, synchronicities, and gifts
amped up.

For example, the surgery is performed
in the same hospital where I was born
in Atlanta, Georgia.

The surgeon's office manager's daughter
happens to be best friends with my second cousin,
which resulted in an *extraordinary* discount
on a surgery that my insurance would not cover,
and my generous family and friends
footed the rest.

Besides the physical benefits of having this surgery,
soulful benefits were hinted at as well,
especially in regard to my relationship with the demon.

Entering my Wounds
and refusing the demon's bait
during my fetus soul retrieval
was the beginning of our separation.

But getting his influence
out of my *body*
apparently took, well, surgery.

In fact, it felt like I could not embody my soul
with him still marking his territory inside me.

And the only person who had the skills and the spiritual presence
to remove him was an incredibly compassionate Christian surgeon
who, I kid you not, looks like a giant cherub angel.

I didn't have the heart to tell him
that he wasn't just excising endometriosis
from my pelvis,
he was also exorcising an ancient demon.

But more than a demon has been hiding out in my pelvis.
Most of my feelings and trauma from my first life reside there as well.

In fact, during our first pre-op appointment,
my surgeon prescribed some surprising medication
—medication I was not supposed to take via my *mouth*.

When I left his office, I immediately called my friend Sharon:

"Girlfriend, guess what?
My PLPTSD (past-life post-traumatic stress disorder)
is so bad . . . that my *vagina* needs valium."

Her immediate reply: "Can we make T-shirts with that phrase?"

If you don't have friends like this
—friends who make you laugh your ass off,
friends who don't blink at your freak (but add to it),
friends who cheer you on as you venture
into the Wild West of your interior
—then Incarnating is *way* more difficult.

But I digress.
Back to the exorcism.

As exorcisms go, this wasn't an easy one.

Not only did I have to prepare for it by energetically deconstructing
and emotionally psychoanalyzing the complex, intimate relationship
I had with the demon, but I had to own my shadows that match it.

Then the surgery itself,
and my recovery,
kicked my butt.

I woke up in immense pain,
extremely nauseated and way out of sorts.
I feared that I had put my poor body
through something unnecessary.

But then my dear friend Tara,
who had flown in for the surgery,
informed me that the surgeon had taken
high-definition photos of the endometriosis
he had removed from my body.

She held up one such photo and humorously asked,
"Why does a Jew have to be the one to point this out?!"
The photo left no room for interpretation.

The photo was of a thick
black cross
adhered to my pelvic wall.

It was endometriosis
that was now ex(or)cised.

I keep the photo on my iPhone,
just because you never know
who you'll be sitting next to
on an airplane.

If my seatmates show me pictures of their kids,
I show them pictures of my pre-exorcised demon.

[wink]

Retrieving Newborn Sarah

After I returned to the crucifixion and retrieved my fetus fragment,
I felt ready to retrieve Sarah's other fragments as well.

But newborn Sarah taught me
that each fragment is distinct
and required a different approach.

When I return to the birth of Sarah,
I allow myself to experience
the devastating feelings
of rejection and being unwanted.

[deep, shaky breath]

Despite their hurtful reactions to me,
I try to do the correct and conscious thing:
forgive my parents' community.

But my Lady stops me.

She asks me to *feel* newborn Sarah,
who is screaming with pain.
My solar plexus is contracted,
and my front body has collapsed.

My Lady counsels:
Don't act more spiritual than this wound.
Ground into your female body,
and do what you feel *like doing.*
Get Real.

Vertebra by vertebra,
my spine straightens,
and my feminine fire reignites.

I scoop up newborn Sarah
and hold her howling body close to my own
so she can feel the solidity of human touch,
the physical presence of my love,
and how much *I* want her.

"I've got you sweet girl, I've got you," I murmur,
my eyes watering, my heart booming.

Sarah settles a bit, but she is still extremely agitated
because she doesn't feel like she belongs in human arms.

I whirl around to face those who are activating these feelings
and then do what any soul mama would do
if this crap were aimed at their baby:
I bitch the disciples out.

"You are acting like a bunch of ASSHOLES!" I yell.
"You are adults! This is a *baby!* A BABY, for Christ's sake!

Take your issues and your negative attitudes elsewhere!
You are not coming near my soul baby again
until you learn how to treat her
with the care and respect she deserves!"

Then I take my soul baby and leave,
slamming the door behind me.

BAM!

That felt good,
Real Good.

I feel empowered as adult Sera
and soothed, protected, and *fiercely* loved
as newborn Sarah.

I discovered that I can take care of myself,
no matter what others throw at me.

I can set boundaries with unhealthy energies and people,
even if they appear or are considered to be "spiritual."

I can walk away, or stand my ground,
or even bitch someone(s) out.

And, even if I didn't or couldn't
do it *then*,
I can do it *now.*

For the first time
I feel safe in my own arms.

Newborn Sarah was back.

That was one of my favorite soul retrievals.

Retrieving Adult Sarah

This next soul retrieval was one of my least favorites.
Retrieving the fragment of adult Sarah
required being buried alive.

I sink down, through the dank earth,
into that dismal and desolate underground room,
and sit next to Sarah.

Learning from my previous retrieval of newborn Sarah,
I allow adult Sarah to be where she is and who she is.
I allow myself to feel what I felt *then*.

As the man who I thought was my friend
rolls that rock over my exit,

air and trust rush out of me,
followed by
the horrendous sensation of rape.

But it's not my body
that has been violated,
it's my soul.

Shock renders me mute and immobile.
With my only source of light missing,
I am swallowed by the hungry darkness.

Not only was I betrayed by someone I trusted,
but I betrayed those who entrusted *me*.

I handed the keys to the Kingdom and Queendom
to a jailor
who does not want anyone to be free.

My lungs collapse
as *what I did*
lands on my chest.

I failed
my Parents,
my Lineage,
myself . . .
you.

My regret is like a rabid animal.

I scramble about in the dark,
frantically searching for some way out,
but my failure fills every crack
and my self-loathing seals every stone.

I scream as loud as I can
for as long as I can,
but nobody hears me.

Nobody has heard me.

I keel over, clutching my arms as I feel
everything that has been done in the name of my father,
without my mother
and without what I was entrusted to pass on.

I feel Christianity's fear
of Natural Ways of Being,
and the resulting near extinction
of Organic Life.

I feel the horrors and the heartlessness
of the Crusades and Holy Wars.

I feel the terror during the Inquisition
when *millions* were tortured and massacred by the Church
for speaking, writing, or living their truth.

I feel the confusion and fright felt by every human
who has been told that they are *going to hell*
because they have not made Jesus Christ their savior.

I feel the sickening physical and psychological self-flagellation
that results from being called or believing one is a "sinner,"

the relentless soul-sucking struggle
to be good enough to "get into heaven,"

and the resulting distrust in and suppression of one's authentic nature,
creative self-expression, and healthy sexual preferences,
which so often leads to depression, disease, addiction, and even suicide.

I feel the lack of self-confidence and the diminishment of power
within all the little girls who are treated as less than little boys.

I hear the millions of silenced female voices
and sense their shut-down, shamed, and defiled bodies
and the interrelated desecration of this earth.

I feel all the women who are trapped
by "the virgin" and "the whore"
instead of respected and released
by the ravishing truth of
both my grandmother and mother.

I feel all the men who have taken a vow of celibacy
in order to be (un)like my father,
and the rampant repression and sexual abuse that has resulted.

I feel the inflation and power-mongering
of many Christian leaders who have overtly or covertly
stolen the spiritual authority away from their followers.

I feel the spiritual abuse committed
by attempting to "save" others,
which denies and dishonors
the Sovereignty of the Soul.

I feel, I feel, and I *feel*
the devastation caused by Christianity

and the incalculable and unnatural wounds
it's inflicted on souls, bodies, and the earth.

[pause]

My scholarly mind is well aware that the Church
isn't solely responsible for everything I listed above,
and that Christianity has also been a *positive* influence.

The Church has been a liberating resource for many,
and has committed outstanding acts of service,
and many Christians throughout history suffered horribly
at the hands of others.

But nothing stalls a soul retrieval faster than intellectual critiques
or psychological analysis of one's honest feelings.

What I needed to stay
true to during this retrieval
was *my wounded soul fragment,*

who, yes, somewhat narcissistically,
felt more than partially responsible
for the negative affects of Christianity
since her lockdown.

I roll back and forth, crying out:
"I'm sorry, I'm sorry, I'm sorry."

I can't stop apologizing.
"I'm sorry" is my soul's mantra
and I have to keep saying it.

Because nothing can fix what I have done,
or repair the damage I believe I have helped cause.

My faults finished my Lineage.
My weakness defeated *Their* Love.
My *humanness* fucked everything up.

My hatred of being human rumbles to the surface,
ironically making me sound not unlike the Church.

Although my confession feels like a release,
it also feels like a life(times) sentence.

As my fractured soul, I am *convinced*
that I belong in this cell forever
and that the world is better off without me.

I exhale and lie face down in the dark.

Almost imperceptibly
the air shifts around me.

I can't see in the darkness,
but I can feel that someone else
is now here, with me.

It is one of you.

I gasp and scuttle away.

The air changes again
as another one of you
arrives in my cell,
then another, and another.

I'm stunned and retreat further against a wall.

Soon, a warm body touches my own.
Then a different body finds me.
There is no more room for me to hide.

The cell is now full.

I panic and feel like I'm suffocating,
but you all start breathing together,
slowly and rhythmically.

inhale . . . . . . exhale . . . . . . inhale . . . . . . exhale.

I begin to breathe with you.

After a while,
I feel connected to you,
supported by you,

and then,

I feel something even more powerful:
I feel forgiven and *loved* by humanity.

My body shudders with release,
and the walls around my heart crack
allowing a truer reality than the one
I've been inhabiting to trickle through:

My Soul's Reality.

Red leaks out of my heart
and into my body.

It flows faster and grows stronger.

As it Refills me, it Reminds me
not only why I Chose to be human,
but why I Chose to be *Sarah*.

I didn't choose to be Sarah
only to expand my capacity to Love
and evolve as a Being,
like I had previously Remembered
before my return to the crucifixion.

This is not an abstract Love
that I am now feeling.
It's personal.

It's an incredibly intimate
experience and expression
of *LOVING*.

It is more Love than I have ever felt,
and it is flowing *from Me*.

It is Red. It is Hot. And it is Holy.
It is Unwavering, Unstoppable Devotion.

I Remember. I Remember. I Remember.

It's because I Love
my Parents, humanity, and this planet,
so fucking much
that I Chose this role of Sarah.

I bow my head and the tears pour.

I chose my life as Sarah
in order to *one day*

be a Living and Loving Reminder
of Who We All Truly Are.

We are the Third.

We are the missing pieces
of
Love's Story.

We are the daughters and sons
of this Universe.

And,
We are Universes Ourselves,
Distinct Divine Souls
Who have dared to become human.

We
Make
True Love
Whole.

I couldn't remind anyone of This
by floating above or by beaming down
as some seraphic blaze of love and light.

For that is not how Organic Life roots
or True Love grows here.

The Reality is:
I wasn't buried.
I was *planted*.

I needed to be placed in the dark earth first
and experience everything that entails

in order to eventually be able to support
my fellow soul sisters and soul brothers
who might feel buried, too.

This is what we do for each other.
This is what you all just did for me.

I compassionately place my hands on my chest.

I did what *any* human fetus
would do during that crucifixion.

I needed to disassociate, fragment, shut down,
and even sell out
in order to protect myself and my body.

My survival instincts saved me.
They did not condemn me.

And then I did the best I could
with that trauma and those core wounds,
in that lifetime and for lifetimes after,
including trusting the wrong people with my truth.

Even feeling abandoned, evil, unlovable, rejected,
betrayed, alone, lost, worthless, and like I failed,
has been an *essential* part of my soul's path.

The Radical Truth is: I didn't fail my mission.
In fact, it looks like I've been doing it all along.

For there is no other way to Incarnate Love
but to go *through* the human experience.

All. The. Way. Through. IT.

And, that is what I am doing.
As are you.

I rub my chest.

My deepest shame has been being human,
but it is actually my greatest triumph.

I wrap my arms around myself.

I've been judging myself so harshly,
for *so* long,
and thereby everyone else as well.

When instead I should be hugging myself,
and everyone else, for being so goddamn human.
In fact, I should be congratulating us all,
because we are obviously really fucking going for it!

Feeling you around me,
I stand up in that cell,

and I forgive myself
and all of you
for being human.

I close my eyes
and start to weep
as what feels like
the Waters of Life
pour over me,

washing me free of all the paradigms and belief systems
that have directly, but more often indirectly, taught me
to feel less than and ashamed for being human.

I am being cleansed of *their* sins.

I am being Baptized
by my Divine Being,
and my Divine Parents,

so my body and soul
can shamelessly enter
the heaven and hell
of humanity.

I open my eyes.

Although it took my father only three days
to roll the stone away from *his* tomb,
I'm not entirely convinced this proves he is stronger.

For it takes a particular kind of strength
to stay in the dark for as long as so many of us have.
It is a different kind of sacrifice.

Sarah's life was a sacrifice.

It was a crucial and auspicious beginning
of my Soul's journey to becoming human.

It prepared me
to be and do
what I originally came here
to be and do:

Love.

Now I have the opportunity to transmute
my personal suffering into support for others
(with no shadowy strings attached).

I have the ability to turn my past
into a genuine present.

It's Time

for many of us
to grow up

and come out of the rich, dark soil.

It's Time

to blossom as shameless, human souls
and reveal our unrefined, natural beauty.

I place my hands on the walls of my cell
and start digging.

Sacred Roles

I dig faster and faster in the soul realm,
making the same bodily motions in the physical realm.
I dig like my life depends on it.

When my fingers find that rock,
I resource all the strength I have gained
from living under it
and break right through it.

And then I'm standing above ground
squinting in the bright sun, covered in dirt.

With a ferocious ROAR I start chasing after
the man who stole my Soul and locked my body away,
my feet pounding in place in physical reality.

When I reach him,
I rip my Redness out of his greedy hands
and swallow it with a voracious gulp.

Belch!

Furiously, I start to dance around him in the soul realm,
and in my bedroom in the physical realm.

My movements are untamed and anarchic.
I stomp my feet and swing my hair.
I stick my tongue out and widen my eyes.
I hiss and growl and make terrifying noises.

I get right up in his face,
and let him know just
who he has messed with:

Sarah-*la-KALI!*

But then, my Holy Feminine Rage
twists into something less liberating:
my human thirst for revenge.

The sudden and savage *need*
to make this man suffer and pay
for his crimes against my body and soul,

my Lineage and the Feminine,
feels almost impossible to resist.

So I ask for help.

My Lady Turns Up:
There is nothing wrong with what you are feeling.
Let him know the pain his actions have caused.
Tell him how you feel.

Through quivering lips and with beads of sweat
rolling down my face, I tell the man what he has done
to me and my loved ones and how much it has hurt.

He stays silent,
eyes wide.

Now sense his reality, my Lady nudges.

I open toward him and begin to feel
how fearful he is of me
and of what I am sharing with the world.

He honestly believes that I am poisoning
his spiritual lineage.

Ending my life and covering up my existence
was not easy for him,
but he felt it was necessary and justified.

As if waiting in the wings, more men
from my parents' community appear.

In this open state, I can feel why my birth upset them so much:
because *they* felt unqualified and unsure
about taking on their beloved teacher's mission!

And because their teacher's only child was born female,
they then felt entirely responsible for doing so.

They didn't realize the effects of their treatment toward me.
I was just a girl to them, and my mother, just a woman.

I felt their wounding around women and fear of the Feminine.
I recognized how their wounds, shadows, and power struggles
allowed the interfering forces, like patriarchy, to work through them,
just like they can work through *all* of us.

My heart softens toward these men,
and I start to release my grip,
which allows me to become aware
of my own accountability.

Truth was, *I* rejected my Soul and my mission in the womb
and then blamed the disciples for rejecting me and my mission
when I came out of the womb.

Deep down, *I* believed I was evil
and then blamed that disciple
for treating me as if it were true.

I didn't want to exist at the end of my first life,
and then I blamed the Church for excluding me
and the whole world for not knowing me.

While admitting this doesn't condone
the cruel or unjust actions of others
—nor is this about self-blame—
it *does* require that I look in the mirror
and take an appropriate amount of responsibility.

It's easier to project the cause of my pain outward
at spiritual authorities and institutions, at the unfair world,
at demons, at those close to me,

than it is to focus inward
and admit that I've done similar things to myself
that I've accused others of doing to me
and I was the first one to do so.

The air starts to clear and my Soul's lens widens,
helping me recognize the Roles that we, as Divine Souls,
play for each other on Earth,

and the challenges and lessons
we provide for one another
that help us grow as human souls.

In other words, there is a *Sacred Role*
the disciples have played for me
by dismissing my Original Role.

Behind the scenes, as Divine Souls,
these men were (and still are) *challenging* me
to let go of my aspirations to prove myself to them
and give up my need to be accepted and respected
by them and all spiritual teachers and authorities

including the Church.

A bitter taste fills my mouth.
I hold more resentment toward the Church
than I do toward *any* other institution.

My Lady carefully asks:
What is the Sacred Role of the Church?
What is it teaching you
by acting in opposition to you?

The answers rush forth:

"By acting as *the* Spiritual Authority,
the Church is, er, 'encouraging' me
to become my own Spiritual Authority

and Know and express *my* Truth,
no matter what spiritual traditions
claim is *The* Truth.

By denying the love shared between my parents,
the Church is provoking me to *Remember* True Love.

By believing my first life is a lie,
the Church is pushing me
to believe in myself!"

Fired up, I can See the Sacred Roles
all my oppositional forces and so-called enemies play,
and recognize the necessary "Boot Camp"
they have provided for me.

My Lady continues,
How you choose to act in response
to someone or something that has harmed you
is what makes your parents' teachings
Come Alive . . . *or not.*

I recall what my father did right before he died
and what my mother continued to do afterward:
They forgave those who harmed them.

Forgiving freed the souls of those who betrayed them,
and it freed my father's and mother's souls, as well.

When we don't forgive,
we stay chained to that person or thing
throughout time,

repeating our patterns
and perpetuating our injuries,

instead of healing from the initial wound
and evolving beyond it.

If we don't forgive,
we hold ourselves
and the other
back.

We obstruct the natural movement of Life.

Forgiveness not only changes us
and those we forgive,
it changes this planet.

Because it is in the act of forgiveness
that we Incarnate Love.

[clearing my throat]

All that said, forgiveness is not another "should"
we need to put on our spiritual "to do" list
and feel guilty about or judge ourselves by.

For most of us, it takes time to forgive
(uh, two thousand years for me),
and some substantial help from our Soul.

Forgiveness doesn't make
what happened right or okay.

Forgiveness does not mean we should forget
or pretend that the harm didn't occur
or ignore how we still hurt from it.

To forgive *requires* that we tell our story,
feel our pain, and voice our violations.

By owning what happened to us,
we are finally able to let it go,
and let Love In.

Our life becomes our own again.

We are no longer defined
by what has happened to us
but instead by the resilient human
we have become as a result.

I take a deep breath and face the disciples and the Church.

"You have been the bane of my entire human existence,
but I now recognize and respect the Sacred Roles
you are playing for my soul and for many souls.

Thank you for all you have taught me
and will continue to teach me.

I forgive you."

With tears in their eyes,
the disciples nod
and walk away.

When the man who locked me underground
walks away from me,
toward the Church he is credited for building,

I can't help but notice how different
his footprints are from my father's.

My Personal Trainer

Immediately, the demon who operated *through*
the man who rolled that rock over me materializes
and looms menacingly.

I fall into my usual position and cower in fear.
This guy is no joke because evil is no joke.

He has abused me and violated me in every way imaginable,
and many ways unimaginable, resulting in severe and what has
felt like permanent damage to my body, soul, energy, and psyche,
and he has committed heinous crimes against those I love.

I feel my Lady's firm hand on my lower back.
I straighten my spine as I receive Her support.

What has the demon been teaching you? My Lady gently asks.

I focus on his Sacred Role in my lives.

Ah.

He's been teaching me
that no matter what it feels or appears like,
no one can steal my mission
or my Soul.

Tears spring to my eyes.

He has taught me about betrayal:
Betrayal by others and of others,
but also *betrayal of my self.*

The hairs raise on the back of my arms.

Through all his antics and abuse,
he has *ultimately* been "training" me
to honor, claim, and embody my soul.

And, are you honoring your Sacred Role with him? My Lady inquires.

Awareness ripples through me,
followed by dumbfounded shock.

I haven't been.

My hatred toward him has chained us together,
preventing us both from becoming free and evolving.

His influence might have kept me buried in darkness,
but *my* lack of forgiveness
was keeping *him* buried in darkness.

Beneath all his terrifying awfulness,
I can sense an infinitesimal desire to change.

A soul spark.
And it is enough.

This seems eerily similar to
when I was stuck in that dark cell.

I needed *your* forgiveness and Love
to be able to find my Soul again.

And now he needs mine.

I step out of the chains binding me,
pick up the heavy links between us,
and start walking around the demon,
unwrapping him layer by layer.

With each circumambulation
I say, "I'm sorry."

When he is unchained by me,
we face each other:

human to demon
and soul to soul.

I confess: "I have not been strong enough
to forgive you and release you
from our bondage, till now.
I apologize, and I hope you can forgive me.

No matter what you have done to me and those I care about,
you still deserve the chance to feel True Love, as all Beings do.

And now you have it.

I forgive you.
I release you.
And I Love you."

The demon throws back his thick head
with a heart-breaking howl.

When his dark eyes meet mine again,
we exchange something that *needs* to be exchanged
after playing such epic roles for each other:

Gratitude.

Then he unfolds his tenebrous wings
and flies away.

For the first time
since I was first a fetus,
I feel free.

A Red footnote:

My psychologically reflexive mind would have preferred
a different ending to that complicated relationship.

You know, where I realize the demon
who has stalked my soul all this time
is actually a shadowed part of *me.*

I could then top that with the spiritual cliché:
"Because we're all One."

But I've been in this Universe for far too long,
and I have too much respect for all the complex Beings within it,
to shortchange their sovereignty by blending us all together
into some easily digestible, cosmic chicken soup,
or by treating them as only byproducts of my psyche.

That's solipsistic and disrespectful
from my Soul's Point of View.
Not to mention dangerous.

Are some demons part of our psyches? Of course!

And what complicates things even more
is that our wounds, shadows, and inner "demons"
are how *actual* demons and interfering forces
infiltrate, affect, and work through us.

It is how and why we can become
temporarily "possessed,"
which we *all* have been at times.

However, just because the earthly and cosmic dimensions host demons, this does *not* give us the right to point fingers and demonize others, nor does the demonic reality let us off the hook from doing our psychological and spiritual work.

Instead, this should motivate us to be clear and compassionate toward ourselves and others who are wrestling with such forces, and to remodel our inner domain so demons don't have as many doorways to enter.

To be extra-strength clear:
Demons are not something to dismiss, befriend, bless, or take on.
Make no mistake about it, they aim to destroy Life.

But like all interfering forces,
they *also* serve a Sacred Purpose
and, when we can manage it,
our respect.

Which is why I now refer to my demon,
as my soul's best Personal Trainer.

BREAK (DANCE) TIME

My Fight

Just because I forgave my adversaries
didn't mean I was going to stop fighting them
—especially the Church.

Fighting against the Church
in some way, shape, or form
has been my lifetimes-long mission.

Your mission does not involve the Church, my Lady drops in.

"Uh . . . then *why* have I come out of my underground cell
if I can't sock it to the Church and champion the Good?!"
I, as my newly unearthed soul fragment, shoot back.

Because that will not heal your wounds or help this world, my Lady responds.
This world needs something different from you.
It needs you.

I pause and consider all my lives since Sarah.

But, who am I if I'm not fighting against opposition
or for what my soul holds Sacred?
Fighting for spiritual justice has become *who I am.*

I rub my head as I realize what this means.
Ceasing my fight means losing parts of my identity.

I have to give up being the victim, the martyr, the heretic,
the outcast, the savior, the freedom fighter,
the rebelle with an unconscious cause

—and those parts carry *a lot* of power.

An image arises of me in an angry mob.
I am shaking my fist and lambasting the Church.
My eyes widen in astonishment.

I've been doing to the Church
what the Church has done to me
and many others!

I've been judging the Church, condemning it, accusing it
of not following the "real" God, and punishing it for its "sins."

I unclench my fists.

"OK, but then how the hell do I deal with oppositional forces?" I ask.
How did your parents handle oppositional forces? My Lady tosses back.

I close my eyes and drop into my heart.

My parents didn't *fight* back.
They didn't *oppose* oppositional forces.

They most definitely rocked and often overturned
the spiritual, social, and political boats,
and they upset many who were abusing power and acting unjust.

But those mighty waves were created by my parents
daring to be themselves and living their truth out loud
and encouraging others to do the same,
not by my parents *fighting* against the system.

There's a big difference
between forcing change
and *being* it.

Not fighting back
kept them on mission
and their souls intact.

It kept them out of the game
and in their hearts.

I bring my hands to my heart.

Fighting *for* my parents
has actually separated
me from them.

Attacking the system, fighting for justice,
or hating on my perceived enemies
—which I've done in a variety of subtle
and not-so-subtle ways for lifetimes—

feeds oppositional forces,
drains my life force,
reinforces my prison,

and distracts me
from my *real* mission.

It keeps me in the game,
and out of my heart.

It distances me from my Soul.

My Lady softly interposes:
You have to want your Soul more
than you want to win your holy war.

My "holy war" against injustice
looks and feels like I'm wearing
the top half of a suit of armor.

I realize that fighting has also been a *defense*
protecting me from what my father went through.

But being naked, vulnerable, with his heart exposed
turned out to be my father's greatest *strengths*.

Despite what it looked like,
the oppositional forces did *not* win
when they crucified my father.

They only win when we close our hearts and stop Loving.

My Lady chimes in:
The Power that comes through
your undefended heart
is a Power
that can never *be taken from you.*

This is *True* Power.
This is Love's Power.
This is our Soul's Fire,
which *never* burns out.

It is not *of* this earth,
but it is *for* this earth.

By leaving the battlefield
we enter the Living Field

and we align with the Force,
which created
this entire Universe.

Putting down our "weapons"
in the face of opposition
might seem like madness to our minds,
but it's sanity to our Souls.

This is *not* martyrdom
or about purposefully putting ourselves
in dangerous situations.

This is also not about bypassing the human reality
because we believe in or understand the Divine Reality.

Becoming fully human
requires holding
both realities
together.

We See the Bigger Picture
and we dedicate ourselves
to the smaller scene.

We sit down and pray
and we stand up and act

not just nonviolently,
but also *Lovingly*,

not only toward our neighbor,
but also toward our enemy.

This is what my mother did.

Although she was hit hard,
she *Loved* harder.

Her husband died for Love,

but *she stayed here*,
right in the thick of it,

and *Lived* for Love.

Living as she did after the crucifixion
is possibly an even *greater* teaching
than my father's.

This is what made my parents a Power Couple.

My parents demonstrated
that no matter what happens
to us, others, or this planet,

We. Can. Still. Choose. Love.

And, when we do,
even if it appears
like the opposite,

Life Wins.

Nothing is lost,
and
Everything gains.

We stay Whole.
And, we sustain
the Whole.

However, there is a "catch:"
Organic Change Takes Time.

We might not see the results
of our brave actions right away.

We might even feel like
we have been beaten or buried.

But what we have actually done
is leave a trail of True Love
for others to follow
in their own footsteps,

and

we have made a deposit of courage
in the earthly account
for others to withdraw from,

and

we have widened
the pathway Home,
here.

Little by little,
lifetime by lifetime,

we stretch ourselves
and this planet open

so more and more
Love pours in.

[heart beat]

I take a deep breath and square up with The Church,
which dominates far more than just *one* religion.

"I have fought you for eons
in both the earthly and the cosmic realms,
and it has done neither of us, or this planet, any good.

It has kept us locked together
and kept Love locked out.

Initially, as a Divine Soul, I wanted to 'play the game'
and have the experience of fighting against you.
And I've needed opposition and so-called enemies
in order to learn and grow as a human soul.

But now I'm ready to try something different.

I'm ready to join my Parents
and stop fighting against
and start *standing for*
Life *as* Love."

I feel all my fighting energy
that has fueled me
for two thousand years,
and I allow it to

build,
and Build,
and BUILD

and then,

I OPEN MY HEART.

BOOM!!!

True Love

After my heart opens,
I am no longer in control.

And that's how True Love finds me.

When It does, my brain short-circuits
because it cannot comprehend
What I am encountering.

But every cell in my body
Recognizes Its Maker.

I fall to the ground.
I had forgotten what True Love
truly was.

It is the precursor to Strength.
It is the prototype of Power.
It is the Genesis of Life.

It is the beating Heart of this Universe,
and *nothing* "beats" That.

While I experienced True Love at the crucifixion
during my fetus soul-fragment retrieval,
it was through my parents' hearts.

Now, I was experiencing True Love
through my own heart.

I haven't had this direct and unfiltered
personal contact with It
since I first entered this Universe.

True Love asks: *Do you trust Me?*

I become excruciatingly aware
of all my agendas and strategies
to *get* Love:

By being spiritual enough.
By helping people.
By looking and sounding and doing right.
By making up for my past mistakes.
By fighting hard enough for It.

By taking down the Church and resurrecting the Original Lineage.
By making my parents proud, and humanity want me, and this world accept me.

By healing my core wounds.
By retrieving and embodying my soul.

By making myself *worthy* of It.

But I can't.

I can't control or manipulate
the Heart of this Universe.

And I don't need to.

Because what I'm Experiencing
in these Moments of All Moments

is that

True Love is *always* Loving us,
no matter what we do or don't do
or who we are or aren't.

Love Does What Love Is.

No one and nothing
can stop Love from Loving.

But we can block ourselves
from receiving and giving
True Love.

I have.

While I can't make myself
be Truly Loved or Truly Love,

I *can* practice letting go
of everything I have put
in True Love's Way,

including all my strategies and agendas.

I can't be a Goddess.
Or an Enlightened Masteress.
Or the immaculate child
of Jesus Christ and Mary Magdalene.

I have to be everything my inflated ego and deflated wounds
and this fixing, perfecting, proving, achieving, winning,
self-helping, enlightenment-seeking, spiritually overambitious
culture resists being.

I have to be *human.*

It's the only Way True Love can Incarnate here.

Through me and as me,
as I am *now.*

Not as I wish myself to be,
or attempt to make myself into,
or believe I need to become.

For it's clear to me,
crumpled up on the floor,
that my imperfection
is True Love's Admission.

In other words, my brokenness
is True Love's entrance.

And, True Love is what brings
all my pieces back together again.

For although we are just as Lovable
lost and scattered about,
we are not meant to stay lost
and scattered forever.

It takes True Love to Forget, Shatter, and Lose Ourselves
and
it takes True Love to Remember, Heal, and Find Ourselves.

All are Astonishing Acts of *Self Love.*

At this point, I'm still on the ground,
trembling and sweating,
and pretty damn sure I don't feel *That:*

Self Love.

And I know I can't make myself Love myself
no matter how important I believe it to be
or how many self-help books I read.

Because really . . .
nothing is in *my* hands.

Everything is in *Love's* Hands.

I have never felt more vulnerable or exposed or humbled.

I have never felt more *human.*

I sputter:
"I'm so sorry for thinking
I know better than You,
and for not trusting You, Love.

I am ready to learn how to trust You again.
I am ready to learn how to Live through You
and allow You to Live through me."

I swallow and continue.

"I Know now that You
have *always* been here
with me and inside me.

You are the Red Beating Heart of me.

Thank you for Reminding me
What You Are, Who I Am,
and Why I am Here.

Thank you for holding
each of us,
and this entire Universe
Together.

I Love You, Love."

True Love increases Its Presence,
charging up my cells and rushing through my veins;
then It fades away from my immediate awareness.

I slowly peel my drenched body off the floor
and feel my Lady's heated Presence.

There is something else you need to face.

I raise my hands in surrender.

My Lady lovingly turns me around as Sera,
to face my soul, Sarah.

Reclaiming Sarah

Hell hath no fury like a scorned soul.

Sarah whips around me
like a tornado,
tearing everything apart.

I duck for cover, but she screeches,
"Look at me! Look at what you have done to your soul!"

She is pale with dark circles under her lifeless eyes.
Ragged black robes hang off her emaciated body.

"You continue to reject me!" Sarah shouts.
"You doubt and deny me!
You make me feel unworthy of Life!"

I gasp and feel like I'm going to be sick
as the truth of what Sarah is shouting
punches me in the stomach.

While I had merged with and retrieved Sarah's soul fragments,
I had yet to reclaim Sarah as the essential part of *my soul.*

Sarah takes a step closer.

"*You returned to the past in order to live freely in the present.*
You have allowed yourself to feel lifetimes of repressed pain.
You are releasing trauma from your body and healing your core wounds.
You are retrieving and integrating previously lost and fractured parts of yourself.
You are forgiving those who have harmed you.
You are dropping your weapons and opening your heart.
You are Remembering True Love."

Sarah raises her hand and jabs a thin finger at me.

"*And yet you think your experiences of me are 'crazy'!*
When what's actually 'crazy' is living without your soul!

You need your soul to be complete,
to contribute your gifts to this planet,
to feel Alive and to Incarnate True Love!

Soul loss is an underlying reason why humanity
and this planet are in such dire straits!
Doing what it takes to embody your soul is a Public Service!"

"Hold on, Sarah!" I cut in.

"I'm not exactly afraid to embody my soul,
I'm freaked out by *who* my soul claims to be!

Who you are, Sarah, not only bitch slaps the face of history
and challenges the largest religion on the planet,

but *What* you represent
as the missing Soul
in the Original Trinity,

contradicts what most people have been taught to believe is 'God,'
and it implies that almost every spiritually sanctioned higher realm, end goal,
or ultimate state, such as Source, Oneness, Nondual Awareness,
Unity Consciousness, and enlightenment

are cosmic buffers
to Organic Reality
and purposeful decoys

en route to

Remembering and Reclaiming
our Distinct Divine Identity!

So, there's also THAT!"

"*EXCUSES!*" Sarah roars.
"*These are just 'spiritual' excuses
for why you can't be yourself!*"

Another truth bomb goes off in my belly
and I bend over, heaving,
as my history of self-rejection overwhelms me.

I have rejected *both*
my Divine Soul, the Red Lady,
and my human soul, Sarah,

because they don't match
collectively agreed-upon
spiritual realities.

While I have made amends with my Red Lady
and brought Her into my public life,
I'm still keeping Sarah locked underground.

My biggest fight is no longer (and perhaps never was)
with the Church, my demon, or oppositional forces.
It is with *myself.*

I am the Inquisition.

I'm oppressing Sarah in order to fit in, be liked,
and not make others uncomfortable
or upset the spiritual status quo.

I'm more worried about what people will think and feel
(you, my family, my publisher, my colleagues)
than what my soul thinks and feels.

But each time I reach outside of myself
for acceptance, I let go of my soul's hand.

And Sarah is abandoned
once again.

Sarah takes another step closer to me.

"*No matter how many people like you,
or how big your career or spiritual consciousness grows,
or how much you help others and this world,*

you will never be whole,
you will never be fully human,
you will never be truly you
WITHOUT ME!"

Sarah steps even *closer,*
till we are almost touching,
and hoarsely whispers:

"I'm so tired of being alone, Sera.
I want to come home now."

She wraps her thin arms around herself
and starts to sob.

My body is aching with Sarah's pain,
but. I. just. can't. do. this.

I'm astonished by how strong my refusal is to claim Sarah.

It feels childish and obstinate,
traumatic and tender.

It's multifaceted and merged with my musculature.
It changes texture and shape with each movement I make.

It stretches back through time and forward into my possible future
collecting every piece of evidence it can find,
building a solid and convincing case why I should *not* claim Sarah.

It scrambles my mind and scaffolds my emotions,
creating confounding and countless layers
between my inner reality and the world's reality.

Like, what the fuck does it mean if I *do* claim Sarah?

Does it mean I'm announcing to the world
that I'm the reincarnated daughter
of Jesus Christ and Mary Magdalene?

Am I really going to be *that* woman?

I can already imagine the cynics and jokes.
I mean, *I* wouldn't take that woman seriously.

I can also envision my future inbox filled with earnest emails
from "long-lost reincarnated family members or friends,"
and public events where people project all their shit or shine onto me.

Or worse, what if someone acts violently toward me or those I love?
Few things madden people more than when their spiritual beliefs are threatened.

It all makes my skin want to crawl right off my body.

And how can I be sure that what I'm sharing is *true*?
There is nothing outside of me that can confirm anything
that I have experienced inside of me.
What if I'm wrong? What if this is *just* my psyche gone wild?

I drop my head as my chest caves in.

I feel lonely and weird enough as it is;
claiming Sarah feels like it will isolate me
even more.

I raise my head as my chest puffs out.

Why can't I just be *me*?
Plain ol' Sera Beak is good enough!

I don't need to latch onto some sensational
—and possibly fabricated—figure from the past

in order to validate or ruin myself
and my mission in the present!

Fuck that!

There are *far* better ways to help this planet
than to claim Sarah!

My Lady interrupts:

What if reclaiming Sarah
is why *you were born*
and how *you can best help this planet?*

I instantly restock my refusal with new ammunition:

"Then why can't I reclaim her in *private*?!

Remembering and writing Sarah's story was healing for *me.*
Why publish this book for others to read?! How will this help them?
Or why can't I at least make the book fiction or Jungian
and frame it as an example of active-imagination therapy?!"

I vigorously shake my head,
"I just don't understand why
I have to go public with Sarah
like *this.*"

Silence is my Lady's answer,
giving me the space to find my own.

Abruptly, my heart slaps my head.

THWACK!

And the Reality blazing
behind this book's reality
Reveals Itself:

True Love
in the form of
Self Love.

My hands find my chest
as my butt finds the floor.

Publishing this book
is a *demonstration*
of Love
for my soul.

Taking this risky and seemingly "crazy" leap of faith
shows my soul that *I* trust her and *I* believe in her.

Claiming my soul when the world has disclaimed her
is the Grand Finale of my soul's retrieval,
and publishing this book is the perfect Setup for our Reunion.

Going public with my experiences
provokes my greatest fears, exposes my core wounds,
reactivates my trauma, triggers every loose part of me,
precisely stimulating my predisposition of self-abandonment,

thereby, offering me chance after chance to do
what I haven't been willing or able to do in the past:

Embrace my Soul.

The tectonic plates of my Being suddenly shift.

Holy Fuck.

It's always been about This.

It's never been about proving Jesus and Magdalene's marriage,
saving the Lineage, or some "big mission."

Loving and accepting myself *is* my mission.
It's *how* I carry on the Lineage!
It's my Redvelation!

My body catches Fire with my Truth.

This book is *not* about a woman claiming
to be the reincarnation of Jesus and Magdalene's child!

This book is about a woman reclaiming *her own soul*!

Sarah is more than a person from a previous life
or a soul fragment.

Sarah is the *timeless essence* of my soul

who is

the daughter of Jesus and Magdalene,
and the daughter of this Universe.

The difference between these perspectives anchors me
and reminds me of my Soul's Choice to be Sarah.

Withholding my soul from the world
is withholding my support and love
for other souls and my Parents.

It's doing the same thing that
I've accused the Church of doing:
tampering with the Original Trinity.

Reclaiming Sarah
means reaccepting
my Original Role

and rejoining
my human
and holy family.

It means being the Third,
like we *all* are,

which requires
that I live and share
my truth

here in this Universe,
here on this planet,
and here in this book.

I turn toward my raggedy, withered soul
who has been watching patiently from the sidelines.

I look her straight in the eyes,
and with all my heart I apologize:

"I'm so sorry, Sarah.
I am *so* sorry for what I have done to you."

She stares at me, warily.

"*I don't know what to do with all my pain*," she quietly states.
"Give it to me, Sarah. For I am the one who has caused it," I answer.

She does.

Years ago, I felt the pain of abandoning
my Divine Soul, the Red Lady.

Now I was feeling the pain
of abandoning my human soul, Sarah.

It's the worse pain I have ever felt.

It's the kind of pain that comes forward
when you finally admit
that you have left yourself behind.

I'm sitting on the ground,
legs bent behind me,
forcing myself to breathe.

Every part of me
feels like it is hurting
every other part of me,
until all I am is

HURT.

I grow dizzy and sway,
my legs slip beneath me.

And then,
like a tornado,
it passes.

Leaving just me.

But it looks and feels like
I'm restrained
by two thousand straightjackets.

I can't move, and I can barely breathe.
I panic and struggle to escape this bound position
that I have kept my soul in for so long,
but it is useless.

I feel my heart beating against the constraints
and become aware that it was specifically designed
to handle this sort of thing.

It's all the muscle I need.

ba boom, ba boom, ba boom

I follow its bold lead
and make a bold decision:

to accept and love myself
for abandoning my soul.

My heart beats louder
and grows bigger and brighter.

*ba **boom**, ba **boom**, ba **boom***

With each encouraging heartbeat
I decide to accept and love myself
a little more,

ba Boom

and more,

Ba Boom!

and even more,

Ba Boom!!

My heart keeps growing
larger, stronger, and Redder,
pushing, pushing, pushing
against the straightjackets:

Ba BOOM!! Ba BOOM!! Ba BOOM!!

Until finally my soul's bindings *explode*

BOOM!!!

and there are no more self-imposed layers
between me and the outer world.

I am unbound and undefended.
A human heart, fully exposed.
A Red soul, set free.

I open my swollen, soaked eyes
and Sarah is standing in front of me
with fire in her eyes and roses in her cheeks.

Her mangy black robes have changed
into magnificent red-and-gold folds.

She is glowing.

She has filled out her flesh
and found her heart.

She has Come Back to Life.

She takes off her robes,
revealing her naked body,
and showcases the "battle" scars
she has incurred by becoming human.

She has been scarred *for* Life.

I am awestruck by my human soul's Natural Beauty.

She is wounded *and* Whole,
weathered and Radiant,
lined and Sublime.

She is Real.
She is me.

Sarah smiles and steps closer.
We lean in and rub noses.
We giggle.

We raise our hands to hold each other's faces
and stare into each other's eyes.
True Love is our reflection.

We start to do an ecstatic jig around the room,

spinning and jumping,
laughing and crying,
singing and shouting.

Sarah grabs my hand and turns us outward
so we're facing the whole world
Together.

She gets a mischievous look,
cocks her head,
and belts out a line from a
stadium-anthem *Jock Jams* song:

"Y'all ready for this?!"

Then, my soul twirls into my open arms

and I Am Home.

Forward

Forward

I'm moving forward
with my beloved soul.

Each day is a new challenge:
to be in my body, to keep my heart open, to feel,
to connect with others and the world around me,

to do what makes me come Alive,
to love and accept myself *as I am.*

Though my journey to becoming human isn't over,

I Know now
that

NOTHING

is stronger or more powerful
than the human soul.

We all are living proof.

Thank you for braving your own soul's story
and for taking the time to read my own.

Redminders

Before we part pages, I want to offer a few Redminders.

You don't need to do what I have done
in order to embody your soul
and become human.

You might not need to remember
past lives or deal with demons
or relive traumatic events.

Follow your Soul's lead
and the Natural Wisdom
of your body.

Don't rush or force
soul work,
wait and *allow.*

Souls are time-released.
They run on Universal Time,
and there's no way to change *That.*

Take care of yourself.

Reach out to others
for support,
especially with trauma.

Trust yourself.

Stay on your path and in your body.
It is your only way Home.

Speaking of Home,
Honor Our Earth.

Respect
Her
beautiful,
breaking
Body

that is courageously holding the weight
of every dimension in this Universe,

grounding every aspect of divinity
into every particle of matter,

fostering each soul's unique expression,
experience and evolution,

and taking an *enormous* beating for it all.

Connect with Her,
support Her and feel Her support of you,
and Love Her.

She is the Ground
of Life.

Reach inside yourself.

What awaits in your depths
is more glorious, wise, and powerful
than anything or anyone outside of you.

Don't be dazzled by cosmic charms
or swayed by spiritual light shows.

The *real* spiritual heroes and heroines
are right here on this planet,
swearin' and sweatin' it out together.

Only Weighty Divine Beings (like you)
have the guts to lose their divinity
and then find it again
through their humanity.

Remember,

your humanness proves your holiness.

Your imperfection is your superpower.
Your soul's bruises are badges of honor.

Your wounds hold your gifts.
Your feelings are your healings.

Your pain reflects your devotion
to experiencing and expressing
all of Life.

Your brokenness demonstrates
your determination to Love
and affirms your ability to Love
and be Loved.

Just sayin'

you are enough
as you are *now*.

More than enough.

You are all this world needs.

And if you feel the nudge from your Soul
to dive even deeper inside yourself,
face and feel your core wounds,
release trauma from your body,
retrieve lost fragments,

and perhaps even go backward
so you can move forward,

then I hope this book offers you
support and encouragement
to Go There.

Which brings me to my next Redminders:

You have the right and natural ability
to Remember your evolutionary path
through this Universe and on this planet.

Your Soul's intrepid journey *should* be honored.

You have the right and natural ability
to reconnect with your Divine Soul
and recollect your human soul,

thereby accessing your Soul's vast
experiences, perspectives, gifts,
Wisdom and Love,

and you have a Sacred Duty
to share your Soul with the world
in ways that feel most authentic to you.

In fact, if you get anything from this bloody book,
I hope it's the importance of embracing and living
your own Soul's truth no matter what others think.

Doing so is an Act of Self Love,
which helps humanity grow
and this entire Universe evolve.

In other words: you have your own Revelation.
In Red words: you *are* your Revelation.

Keeping It Real

Life does not necessarily get easier or "better"
when we embody our soul and become human.
Our problems and struggles don't disappear.

But we *do* get to:

feel at Home in our body,

experience this whole world
through our hearts,

and finally

just
fucking
finally

Be Ourselves

here.

Embodying our soul also directly
and intimately reconnects us
with the Soul of this Universe,

which provides us with everything
we need to help transform this planet.

In other words,
we can help save this planet
if we save our own soul.

If we are privileged enough to have a roof over our head,
food on the table, a semi-healthy body,
and if our life is not in danger,
then we have the means

to do what we can
to become a beacon of Organic Light
on this hurting planet,

extending ourselves to souls in need,
reminding them that they are not alone
and that we are here to support them.

I can guarantee that those tossed about
in the rough, stormy seas now
have been our lighthouse keepers previously.

This is how we souls rotate and operate.
Because none of us can do this alone.

That's right, *each* of us is starring in
the greatest Love Story
ever co-created . . .

and it is far from over.

Moving Forward

I don't know what the future holds,
but I'm open to the evolution of my experiences
as well as the ongoing mystery.

What I do know

is that the more I embody my soul
the more I experience my Truth:

I am my Lineage's Holder.

I am True Love's Living
Human Reminder.

I am here to Remember and Reclaim
my Red Soul
and Incarnate True Love.

I am here to remind you
to Remember and Reclaim
your unique Soul
and Incarnate True Love,

and *Together* we will Reclaim
our Rightful and Beloved
Place within the Trinity.

It's Time.

Real Life

I'm bent over at the waist, laughing so hard my ribs hurt and my eyes leak.
My heart feels so big that I swear it's beating outside my body.

It's the last night of my weeklong Soul Fire retreat,
and we are on a break from the Closing Ritual.

The raucous room is in a celebratory state of disarray,
filled with feathers, rose petals, dirt, leaves, glitter, chocolate wrappers,
miscellaneous items of clothing, strewn cushions, tipped-over water bottles,

and twenty-three sweaty, Soul-Saturated women,
twelve of whom are receiving an impromptu lesson
on how to "twerk" from another participant.

The others are milling about, busy snacking, chatting, hugging, dancing,
and being with each other in a natural and truly loving way.

My two gifted and hilarious friends who make up the soul-support team
are next to me discussing important things such as the reality of
Soul hangovers, tomorrow's breakfast, and if there is enough toilet paper left.

The doors are wide open,
welcoming the warm, fragrant mountain air
and a symphony of crickets, frogs, and goats.

I sense my first parents' presence
and feel their delight and admiration of us all
(my mother's especially with the twerking).

In this moment, after this week,
where each of these brave women
embraced and embodied their Soul,

(all of whom make Jesus and Magdalene's daughter
just another kid on the spiritual block)

I Know in every cell of my body
that we really can do This:

Incarnate True Love.

And more than that,
we *are* doing It.

A few weeks later, I'm eating dinner with my
remarkable, supportive, and loving present parents
who are respectfully asking me about my past parents
and then making hilarious jokes about what to tell their Church group.

A few weeks after that I'm hugging
my heroic, big-hearted partner
as my two dogs wriggle against my legs
and my parrot squawks, "Sera, I love you . . . nice ass."

And there are bills to pay and dishes to clean
and delicious food to eat and neighbors to meet
and jokes to tell and arguments to be had
and friends to call and stories to share
and mistakes to be made and lessons to be learned
and more trauma to heal and feelings to feel
and shadows to own and retrievals to mine
and beaches to dance on and bodies to love
and tears to shed and joy to be expressed
and
so,
so,
so much gratitude to be felt . . .

for being Alive.

Acknowledgments

I could not embody my soul or birth this book without the support of so many incredible people. Words can't convey the depth of my gratitude, but I hope you can feel my heart beating through them.

My extraordinary, supportive, and truly loving family. Dad: For your open-hearted acceptance and unwavering support of me no matter what. Mom: For your deep listening, ongoing nurturance, encouragement of my creativity, and wisdom. Elizabeth: For your compassionate heart, exceptional gifts, and boundless care for the earth and humanity. Caroline: For your fierce love, soulful loyalty, powerful intuition, and inspiring creation and appreciation of beauty. Keat: For your generous heart, spectacular humor, surgery support, and for making my sister so happy and my amazing niece and nephew. Georgia: For your exquisite heart, magic, soulful sensitivity, and true beauty. Weston: For your tender heart, snuggles, mischievous ways, and soulful strength. (And Kimdog and Waverly!) Thank you all for having my back; accepting me as I am; not letting me take myself to seriously, but seriously enough; teaching me to be a better human; and for having the best senses of humor and feeding me such delicious food my whole life. I love you all so very, very much.

Mark: My partner and soul's champion. Thank you for your multidimensional support, patience, protection, brilliance, nourishing meals, and endless grocery store runs. You were the first to read this book, feel Sarah's truth, and receive it in your heart, all of which gave me the courage to share it with others. No one will ever know how intense this process was except for you who have valiantly kept watch during my deep dives, stayed by my side in the roughest waters, and danced joyfully with me each time I made it back to the surface clutching another piece of myself. Our souls share an ancient love and a noble truth that no storm can ever destroy. I love you.

Gail and Henry: Your beautiful condo over the marsh and home in Atlanta, Hana (and Patra), Meow Meow, Fierce, the POS, Henry's meals, and Gail's shamanic work served me in more ways than there are words. Thank you so much for your incredible support and generosity and for providing a safe space for my soulbody to write and heal . . . and for allowing me to come back even after that leaky pipe under the sink. I love you both.

Tara and Judah: How do I thank you both for everything you have given me over these years? Tara, your grounding, healing presence during the surgery; your astonishing gifts, profound insight, and miraculous Soul Fire Retreat support; our many hilarious trips together and nourishing three hour phone calls—my gratitude for our friendship is immense and ongoing. Judah, your unfailing down-to-earth-yet-coming-from-the-center-of-the-universe wisdom, your more than generous help with the edits, your gentle guidance during my (many) freak outs, and all the soothing nature videos and supportive texts. I feel beyond grateful that you both are in my life (again) and that this planet gets to experience your Souls' many gifts. I love you two.

Jessica: Where did you come from, woman? Wait, I know. And I'm so grateful you are with us all again sharing your courageous, enormous heart, staggering organic gifts, and Soul's Magic. There are so many ways you have generously supported me over these years: scooping me up off the ground at the Soul Fire Retreat, feeding me bacon, offering warrioress wisdom and protection (including kicking major demon ass), helping me (finally) match the book's introduction with my soul's truth, building my website, and having an astonishingly accurate spiritual bullshit radar. This planet is lucky to have you, and I am honored to call you, Sean, and the pups (and the noble Josie), true soul friends. I love you, woman.

Mercedes: For your deep and spacious holding, insightful texts, ready sense of humor, TV show suggestions, mac 'n' cheese nods, and remarkable gifts of body and being healing. I'm blessed to have you as a friend who has been through two of these book births.

Anne: For your soul-sister support and ancient creative brilliance; afternoon teas; flower essences; and heart-opening, hands-clapping gifts for the Red Tent and my Red soulbody. It's a Gift to know you and to watch with awe as your gifts emerge more and more, inspiring this entire world with your spectacular Gold-Green Beauty.

Shannon and Eric: For the hilarious t-shirt ideas, the crazy wisdom, and for driving across the entire country and showing up right when I needed you the most. Thank you for your ongoing soulbody support, inspiring love partnership, and for bravely and continuously doing the Real Work for Her and Him, this planet, and all of us.

Briana R.: My Sacred Patron and soul sister. I will never forget the first time I looked into your bright blue eyes in Montana and felt the depth, love, and power of your Soul. Woman, your multifaceted support has more than helped make this book, my mission, and my soul's embodiment happen. You have given me many gifts, including the much-needed gifts of security, nourishment, and wise council, but most of all you have given me the sacred reminder that I am worthy of being supported during this process, as all souls are who dare to share their truth and unique gifts. My gratitude comes from all corners and curves of this Universe, as does my love.

Kristine Backes: For the mountainous presence you are in my life and on this planet, for your soul support, monthly generosity, and your authentic healing gifts.

Ana Strauss: For your courageous, cancer-kicking, glittery, compassionate awesomeness; the text memes that made me laugh out loud during the hardest book contractions; and for my beautiful hair. You are an inspiration, and I can't wait till one of us owns a farm or we take that world tour of weirdly cute animals.

Soul Fire Retreat Women: Thank you all for so bravely and exquisitely showing up in this world and for daring to Know, Embrace, and Embody your Soul. Each one of you inspires me and held the circle for me during this birthing process. I love you all.

Gregory Perron: For your divinely timed emails filled with inspiring poetry, music videos, and fiery-hearted support. I'm honored to know you and call you a soul brother.

Paul Schmidt: For being such a wonderful source of support and encouragement for my spiritual explorations and expressions since I was a child, and for your excellent advice for this book.

Paulo: Thank you for being an awesome soul brother and neighbor and for delivering the line I most needed to hear that one rough day: "The only way to get this wrong is to not do it at all."

Jeff Kripal: For welcoming my Redness in graduate school and up to this very day. Your kindness and support of us mutants and mystics is unfailing and your brilliant work in the world is an ongoing inspiration. Julie Kripal: For your care, delicious meals, and for sharing your powerful healing gifts with me.

Marion Woodman: For doing the work before any of us knew there was soul work to be done and for providing me with the most necessary shakedown of my life. Your fierce commitment to our soulbody's wisdom and voice has forever changed humanity.

Susanne Bersbach: My beloved therapist who is now dancing and laughing in the other realms. Thank you for being there after Marion. For seeing me, holding me, modeling the fiercely compassionate feminine, and supporting my soulbody in more ways than I can name. You are dearly missed.

Robert Rabbin: For your generous help so many years ago and for reminding me of the holy necessity of speaking and writing truthfully. You are dearly missed, but your wise and loving presence on this planet is everlasting.

George Kavassilas: Thank you for bravely speaking your truth, sharing your extraordinary experiences, championing the Soul's Reality, and inspiring me to do so as well.

Peter Levine and Irene Lyon: I didn't explore your work until after my soul retrievals, but I'm grateful for your revolutionary insights and profound contributions regarding trauma and the body.

Lisa Braun Dubbels: For being my unflinching, real deal, hilarious, ridiculously generous, supremely supportive publicist/friend for a decade now . . . and for the bunny pics. Thank you, thank you, thank you.

Haven, Tami, Leslie, Christine, Lindsey, and the amazing team at Sounds True: I cannot imagine any other editor or publisher for this book. Thank you for taking a risk and helping me share my soul's truth with the world. Thank you for not only sounding true, but for Being True.

Endorsers: Judah, Jacob, Jonas, Mirabai, Russ, Lissa, and Lisa: Thank you for your important and meaningful work in the world and for taking the time and heart to support mine. It's an honor sharing this planet with you.

The Center for Endometriosis Care, Debbie, and Dr. Sinervo: For your angelic kindness, heart, generosity, and the healing work you provided for me and so many female soulbodies.

Sacred Donors, I am grateful to all of you who have donated to me over the years so I could birth this wild red soul baby: Mom and Dad, Caroline and Keat, Briana, Jessica, Tara and Judah, Kristine Backes, Philip Corkill, Paola Borgia, Amy Pfaelzer, Tammy Greene, Nadya Vila, Morgan McDonald, Regina Gelfo, Kimberly Smythe, Brittany Nohra, Bethany Butzer, Elizabeth Kupferman, Michael Slack, Margaret Smith, Jennifer Israel, Juliet Oberding, Rebecca Britton, Preeta Banerjee, Maha Naim, Gena Odland, John Lingard, Elizabeth Ellis, Juliet LeBlanc, Alana Grainger,

Anida Wehi, Lejla Marinko, Diana Rae (Rae), Jaqueline Thomas, Addy Heckert, Jakub Edward Checinski, Marina Heinrich, Jessica Lang, Judith Kunkle, Robert Rabbin, Kim Albano de Barros, Vanessa Vazquez, Ann Hughes Ryan, Elizabeth Starr.

My past parents, community, adversaries and allies, personal trainers, relationships, Allison, Rachel, Simmin, Oliver, my dogs Hermes and Lala, my parrot Anaya, Fierce (the five-pound Chihuahua of Simmons Pointe), the Houston neighborhood of Montrose and its Oak trees, the Holy City of Charleston, The Lowcountry, the eagles, wood storks, dolphins, coyotes, pluff mud, Angel Oak tree, Sullivan's Island beach, the Atlantic Ocean, and Papa Sun and Mama Earth.

You: Many times during this multi-lifetime process I didn't think I would make it, but then I would feel you out there—courageously living your own Soul's journey—and it helped me keep going. Thank you for Being Yourself and for doing your Wild Thang with me.

The Lineage: [fist pump]

True Love: **BOOM!!!**

About the Author

Sera Beak is a world-traveled, Harvard-trained scholar of comparative world religions and author of *The Red Book: A Deliciously Unorthodox Approach to Igniting Your Divine Spark* (2006) and *Red Hot and Holy: A Heretic's Love Story* (2013). She offers talks, private sessions, and retreats focused on the radical reality of the Soul and its messy, beautiful love affair with being human. She has a strong affinity for animals, bloopers, subtle realms, and swear words. For more, visit serabeak.com.

About Sounds True

Sounds True is a multimedia publisher whose mission is to inspire and support personal transformation and spiritual awakening. Founded in 1985 and located in Boulder, Colorado, we work with many of the leading spiritual teachers, thinkers, healers, and visionary artists of our time. We strive with every title to preserve the essential "living wisdom" of the author or artist. It is our goal to create products that not only provide information to a reader or listener, but that also embody the quality of a wisdom transmission.

For those seeking genuine transformation, Sounds True is your trusted partner. At SoundsTrue.com you will find a wealth of free resources to support your journey, including exclusive weekly audio interviews, free downloads, interactive learning tools, and other special savings on all our titles.

To learn more, please visit SoundsTrue.com/freegifts or call us toll-free at 800.333.9185.

SOUNDS TRUE
many voices, one journey